BRITISH NUCLEAR WEAPONS
For and Against

JEFF McMAHAN

Preface by Bernard Williams

JUNCTION BOOKS   LONDON

© 1981 Jeff McMahan

© 1981 Preface Bernard Williams

First published in Great Britain by
Junction Books Ltd
15 St John's Hill
London SW11

ISBN 0 86245 0470 (hard)
     0 86245 0497 (paper)

British Library Cataloguing in Publication Data

McMahan, Jeff
    British nuclear weapons.
    1. Atomic weapons 2. Great Britain — Military policy
    I. Title
    355'.0335'41   UA647

Printed and bound in Great Britain by
Whitstable Litho Ltd., Whitstable, Kent

CONTENTS

Acknowledgements   v

Abbreviations   vi

Preface   *Bernard Williams*   viii

I   Preliminaries   1

Introduction   1
The Weapons   2

II   Arguments for the Retention of Nuclear Weapons   13

The Second Centre Argument and the Last Resort
    Deterrent Argument   14
The Trigger Argument   29
    The Tactic of Mere Escalation   32
    The Tactic of Deception   36
The Free-Rider Argument   39
The Problem of Nuclear Blackmail   40
Arguments Concerning Prestige and Influence   47
The Top Table Argument   52
The Multilateralist's Argument   55
The Problem of Germany   62
The Contribution to NATO Argument   65

**III Arguments for the Abandonment of Nuclear
       Weapons**   68

Alternatives to Reliance on Nuclear Weapons   68
    Stronger Conventional Defences   71
    Protection for Military Assets   73
    Civil Defence   75
    'Unconventional Defences'   80

The Soviet Threat   85
The Economic Argument   91
The Prudential Argument   94
The Dangers of Retaliatory Deterrence   104
Against Cruise Missiles   107
Nuclear Weapons as a Source of Provocation   110
The Analogy with Proliferation   112
The Force of Example Argument   116
The Top Table Overturned   118
Moral Arguments   119
Better 'Red' or Dead?   125

IV   **Summary and Conclusion**   130

American Forward-Based Systems   130
NATO Theatre and Tactical Nuclear Weapons   133
Independent Strategic Nuclear Weapons   136
Conclusion   151

Notes   153
Index   163

ACKNOWLEDGEMENTS

Various people have read and provided valuable comments on earlier drafts of this book. I am very grateful to Jonathan Glover, Robert Neild, Derek Parfit, Sir Martin Ryle, Paul Seabright and Bernard Williams for providing me with extensive and detailed comments and suggestions. In particular, I am indebted to Derek Parfit and Paul Seabright for persuading me that the problem of nuclear blackmail is more serious than I had initially been inclined to think. I would also like to thank Robert Neild for making available to me while I was revising this book an advance copy of his excellent book, *How to Make Up Your Mind About the Bomb*. Other people who have given me helpful comments and advice are Charles Gurrey, Sally McMahan, Michael Mason, Adam Roberts, and Dan Smith. Finally, I would like to thank my wife Sally for her skilful typing of three different drafts of this book, and for her encouragement and support throughout the relatively short and therefore extremely hectic period of time in which this book was written.

ABBREVIATIONS

ABM	Anti-ballistic missile
ASW	Anti-submarine warfare
BAOR	British Army on the Rhine
CND	Campaign for Nuclear Disarmament
CTB	Comprehensive Test Ban
GLCM	Ground-launched cruise missile
ICBM	Intercontinental ballistic missile
IRBM	Intermediate-range ballistic missile
MIRV	Multiple independently targeted re-entry vehicles
MBFR	Mutual and Balanced Force Reductions
NATO	North Atlantic Treaty Organization
NORAD	North American Air Defence Command
NPT	Non-Proliferation Treaty
PGM	Precision-guided munitions
SALT	Strategic Arms Limitation Talks
SLBM	Submarine-launched ballistic missile
SIPRI	Stockholm International Peace Research Institute
SRBM	Short-range ballistic missile
TNW	Theatre (or tactical) nuclear weapons

This book is dedicated to
CHARLES TRAWICK HARRISON
in grateful acknowledgement of his
guidance over the years

PREFACE

The danger of nuclear war is probably greater now than at any previous time. The accelerating arms race, together with changes in the international scene, continue to 'destabilize' the equilibrium between the major nuclear powers. Moreover, modifications in weaponry and in military thinking have basically altered the way in which the role of nuclear weapons is understood. Although the change may not have been very widely noticed, nuclear planning has moved dangerously away from the straightforward deterrent conception, which obtained for many years, of 'mutual assured destruction', towards policies based on the expectation of fighting a nuclear war and, supposedly, winning it.

In these changed and frightening circumstances, it is essential to think again, as clearly and steadily as we can, about British policy towards nuclear weapons. Some of those who open this book, may, like myself, have taken part in arguments twenty years ago about 'unilateral nuclear disarmament', and some, again like myself, may have been persuaded at that time by arguments against that policy. I believe that I was right, and that the deterrent policies of those days made sense. I do not believe, however, that our present nuclear policies make sense, nor that the situation now is at all the same as it was then. It is a vitally important fact that the issues are new, and that the arguments which are now needed must be new arguments.

Mr McMahan's book faces up to this need in the most rigorous, clear, sober and unprejudiced way. It will not appeal much to people who think that the answers to these questions proclaim themselves simply and loudly from the skies. He takes very seriously, and pursues with complete honesty, the aim of thinking out the consequences and implications of various alternatives open to British policy. Only a total pacifist, it seems to me, would be in a position to ignore these arguments and be sure of his or her position without studying them. Anyone else, whether inclined in favour of or against British involvement with nuclear weapons, must consider the force of the very powerful reasons that are assembled in this book.

Mr McMahan's arguments are sometimes quite complex. Many of them belong to what one commentator, whom he quotes, has called 'the tortuous world of strategic analysis', and some readers may wonder whether the real world would ever actually correspond to the complex 'scenarios' which are invoked in arguments of this kind. The answer to that may well be 'no', but the process of thought, as realistic as one can make it, still cannot be avoided. Any policies whatsoever — including the dangerous policies to which we are presently committed — are based on *some* thoughts about their consequences and the situation they are designed to meet, and it is better that those thoughts should be clear and careful as possible, rather than crassly confused, as quite certainly much thought is that passes for serious discusion of these issues, whichever side it may be on.

Mr McMahan cannot avoid, as he would readily admit, the problem that there is secret information relevant to these issues and not available to the general public. But there is no alternative to doing the best that one can without it, by studying available information in as detailed a way as is possible for a lay person. Otherwise, one surrenders the right to reach conclusions on these questions to the authorities — authorities who in Britain more than in many democratic countries are secretive and complacent, and who are no more likely than those of other countries to have a correct answer. To give up the right to try to reach clear-headed conclusions about nuclear warfare would be to give up the right to try to think as best we can about literally, our life or death, and there can scarcely be any democratic right deeper than that. In helping us to exercise that right, Mr

McMahan's book makes an important, realistic, and disquieting contribution.

Bernard Williams
Cambridge
July 1981

I
PRELIMINARIES

Introduction

Most people who have studied the problem are agreed that
the danger of nuclear war is now greater than it has been in
any previous period. Not only is nuclear war more likely to
occur, but also the consequences of its occurring would be
far graver now than they would have been in the past. For
this reason, the current debate concerning nuclear weapons
in Britain is a matter of the utmost urgency and importance.
What is at stake is, literally, national survival. This is acknowledged by persons on both sides of the dispute. Defenders of
nuclear weapons claim that without these weapons we, or at
least our freedoms, may perish, while opponents claim that it
is precisely our having these weapons which imperils our
continued survival.

Given the overriding importance of the problem, it is
surprising that the level of the public debate has remained on
the whole rather low. Arguments in favour of nuclear weapons
tend to take the form of ritual utterances about deterrence,
and are often based on uncritical or exaggerated assumptions
about the nature of the Soviet threat. And arguments against
nuclear weapons tend simply to dwell on the horrors of
nuclear war, or to focus on such considerations as how many
times over each side can destroy the other. Writers on both
sides of the debate are guilty of trying to manipulate people
rather than persuade them. They seek to convert people, not
by engaging their reason, but by playing on their fears.

There is, of course, good reason for people to be afraid. And
it is right to want to shake people out of their complacency

unsophisticated debate.

1

and alert them to the present dangers. But it is irresponsible merely to stir up anxiety and alarm, in the hope that people will be moved to act in ways which will reduce the likelihood of war. Simply to arouse people's fears may accomplish little more than lead people to despair, thereby reinforcing their apathy. Futhermore, experience shows that action guided by fear may actually contribute to the occurrence of what is feared. In the past this has been true of the fear of war.

It is important that people should know the facts, and that they should hear the arguments on both sides of the current dispute about nuclear weapons. In spite of the relative lack of emphasis on rational argument in much of the general literature on this subject, there are serious arguments on both sides. This book is intended as a guide to these arguments. I shall have very little to say about the history of nuclear weapons, and I do not intend to burden the reader with an enormous number of facts and statistics. My aim is instead to provide a reasonably comprehensive survey of the various arguments and to submit them to critical scrutiny. Most of the arguments I shall consider are not original, though the attempt to state them in their strongest possible forms will often involve extending or elaborating them in novel ways.

This book is not intended just for defence experts. It is meant to be read by anyone who is interested in the problem of British nuclear weapons or worried about the threat of nuclear war. It is intended as a contribution to a wider public debate which, it is hoped, will permit people to act, not just out of fear, but on the basis of a clear and rational understanding of both the problems and their proposed solutions.

The Weapons

The arguments I shall consider are concerned with whether Britain should retain or abandon certain types of nuclear weapon which it already has, and with whether Britain should acquire or refrain from acquiring certain new types of nuclear weapon. It should be stressed, however, that the arguments are concerned with what Britain should do on the assumption that the Russians' dispositions and behaviour are going to remain roughly the same. Everyone concedes that Britain should give up nuclear weapons if everyone else is also going to give them up; but the question which these arguments address is whether or not Britain should give up certain nuclear weapons given that other countries either may not or will not do so.

It should be emphasized, moreover, that we are concerned here only with *British* nuclear weapons and weapons owned by the US which are stationed on British soil. When the question of whether or not Britain should have nuclear weapons is being discussed, there is a tendency to confuse British nuclear disarmament with disarmament by all of Western Europe, or even with disarmament by the West as a whole. A good example of this tendency came up during the course of a recent public debate between Jonathan Dimbleby, the television journalist, and Francis Pym, the former Defence Secretary. When Mr Dimbleby cited certain arguments against unilateral disarmament by the West as a whole, Mr Pym automatically took these to be arguments against disarmament by Britain. But whether they in fact applied to Britain was an entirely separate and highly controversial question.[1] It is, of course, difficult to isolate the question of British disarmament from that of disarmament by other Western countries, since it might be thought unfair for Britain to disarm if it were considered necessary that some Western countries should have nuclear weapons. I shall return to this question later. For the moment we may limit our attention to Britain.

Of the arguments I shall examine, most apply only to weapons of a certain type or in a certain category, and do not apply to weapons of other types or in other categories. It is rare to find an argument which by itself supports the retention of *all* the nuclear weapons currently operated by Britain, and equally rare to find one — apart from the pacifist argument — which supports the abandonment of all British nuclear weapons. There are, however, particular combinations of arguments which support complete unilateral nuclear disarmament, and other combinations which support a policy of massive nuclear rearmament. And, of course, there are many combinations of arguments which support a wide range

combinations

of options between these two extremes — a fact not always noticed by writers in this area. It is not uncommon, for example, to find an argument brought forward in defence of total unilateral nuclear disarmament when in fact the argument supports the abandonment of only one particular type of nuclear weapon. Similarly, arguments in favour of a single type of nuclear weapon are sometimes thought to justify the continued possession of the whole range of nuclear weapons systems currently operated by Britain.

It is necessary, therefore, before proceeding to discuss the arguments, to provide a catalogue of the various types of nuclear weapon over which Britain has some control. This will allow us to be clear about the implications of particular arguments for particular weapons. The descriptions of the various weapons may be somewhat tedious, but they will prove important for later arguments.

The weapons relevant to my inquiry are normally grouped into three categories: 'independent' weapons, NATO weapons, and American 'forward-based' weapons — though the criteria for determining how a weapons system is to be classified are somewhat obscure. A number of questions seem to be relevant to the classification of a particular type of nuclear weapon: Who can authorize or prevent the use of the weapon? Who determines what its functions are, or what its target is? What are its functions, and what is its target? Who operates it? But even the answers to all of these questions do not rigidly determine how a weapon is to be categorized. It is sometimes difficult to tell why a weapon is placed in one category rather than another.

The only weapons that are usually classified as independent weapons are the missiles carried on board Britain's four *Polaris* submarines. These are ballistic missiles (that is, missiles which follow a high-arch trajectory), and are thus referred to as 'submarine-launched ballistic missiles' (SLBMs). There are 16 missiles on each boat. As a result of the recent *Chevaline* programme for the 'modernization' of the missiles' front ends, each missile now carries multiple warheads. The number of warheads per missile is thought to be between three and six, depending upon whether dummy warheads (for use as decoys) are included. The warheads are not 'independently targetable' and thus would all be aimed at the same target. The missile is designed so that the warheads will separate while approaching the target. They will then land all around the target, thereby increasing the probability that it will be destroyed. (A number of smaller warheads together have more destructive power than a single larger warhead with an equivalent explosive yield.) The main point in having multiple warheads, however, is to be able to saturate and confuse any possible enemy defences.

The *Polaris* force is usually referred to as Britain's 'independent strategic deterrent'. Although these submarines are in fact assigned to NATO command, they are said to be 'independent' largely because Britain retains the prerogative to use them without consulting the NATO allies in the event that 'Her Majesty's Government may decide that supreme national interests are at stake'.[2] There are, however, many respects in which the *Polaris* force is dependent on the US. Although the *Polaris* missiles are fitted with British-made re-entry vehicles and nuclear warheads, the missiles themselves are supplied by the Americans. The force therefore depends on the US for spare parts, rocket fuel, and perhaps even for major maintenance work. Materials used in the production of the warheads have also been obtained from the US, and Britain is entirely dependent on US facilities for the testing of the warheads.

The most important areas of dependence, however, are those which might constrain Britain's ability to use the *Polaris* forces independently. First, the navigation equipment for the submarines was purchased from the US, and it is assumed that the submarines make use of American navigation satellites in determining what their positions are. This is important since, as one writer notes,

> any even minor degradation of navigating accuracy which might occur as a result of not collaborating with the US would be a serious matter; the accuracy with which a SLBM using only inertial navigation can be directed towards a target depends critically on knowing exactly not only where the target is but also where the [submarine] is when it fires.[3]

What this means is that, if for some reason the British sub-marines are denied the use of American navigation satellites, their ability to hit their assigned targets may be seriously impaired.

Another crucial area in which Britain may have to rely on the US is in the gathering of information on targets in the Soviet Union and on Soviet missile defences. Insofar as the relevant information must be obtained by satellites, Britain is to that extent dependent on the US. Just how dependent Britain is in this area is not publicly known, but it would clearly be a major constraint on the independence of *Polaris* if the US were capable of withholding from the *Polaris* commanders vital information concerning targets in the Soviet Union.

Finally, the actual targeting of the *Polaris* missiles is carried out by a NATO group at the US strategic headquarters in Omaha, Nebraska. One writer has commented that this 'is not strictly, however, an element of dependence; given adequate target intelligence ... Britain can certainly target its own missiles if it wishes'.[4] It is important to remember, however, that 'adequate target intelligence' may have to come from the US.

Most writers agree that these various possible obstacles to the independent use of Britain's *Polaris* force could probably be for the most part overcome. But, since all the relevant information on these matters is not accessible to the public, there is certainly room for doubt.

The *Polaris* missiles are classified by the Ministry of Defence as 'strategic' weapons on the ground that they are capable of striking targets within the Soviet Union. (During the 1970s, however, the Pentagon classified the *Polaris* missiles as 'theatre' weapons.) All other nuclear weapons currently owned or operated by Britain are 'theatre' or 'tactical' weapons.

These terms — 'strategic', 'theatre' and 'tactical' — call for some explanation. Unfortunately, there are no agreed defini-tions, and different writers occasionally use these terms in different ways. The definitions I shall offer indicate roughly the way in which the terms are generally understood, and they indicate the way in which I shall use the terms in this book.

'Strategic' nuclear weapons are weapons of intercontinental range, and are normally deployed in the territories of the countries to which they belong (primarily the superpowers), or are carried on board submarines. 'Theatre' and 'tactical' nuclear weapons, on the other hand, are shorter-range weapons which are deployed in regions or 'theatres' of military operations. In the eyes of the superpowers, Europe (or, rather, the non-Soviet part of Europe) counts as a 'theatre'. Theatre and tactical weapons are normally less powerful than strategic weapons, but this is not always true. While some writers take the terms 'theatre' and 'tactical' to mean the same thing, others draw a distinction between them. Certain strategic theorists, for example, hold that 'theatre' is 'the more encompassing term', while 'tactical' is 'the more restrictive'.[5] According to this view, tactical nuclear weapons are 'battlefield nuclear weapons, for battlefield use, and with deployment, ranges, and yields consistent with such use and confined essentially in each respect to the area of localized military operations'.[6] An area of 'localized' conflict is, revealingly, one which is 'away from American or Soviet soil'.[7] Theatre nuclear weapons (TNW) include tactical ones, but also include weapons stationed in military theatres which are of longer range and may be used for retaliatory rather than battlefield purposes.

Britain's theatre nuclear forces are normally classified as NATO weapons. These include several types of aircraft capable of delivering nuclear weapons. Most of these aircraft are, like *Polaris*, independent in the sense that they presumably *could* be used without the consent of Britain's NATO allies in defence of Britain's 'supreme national interests'. But in practice they are even more highly integrated into NATO planning than is the *Polaris* force, and thus they are not normally covered by the phrase 'Britain's independent deterrent'. Another reason for excluding them from the class of independent weapons is that they are less likely than *Polaris* to be *used* independently. They are vulnerable on the ground, and are also fairly old, which means that they would have great difficulty in penetrating Soviet anti-aircraft defences. They are now better suited to 'tactical' roles.

Among these types of aircraft are the old long-range *Vulcan* bombers. As is true of many British nuclear weapons systems, figures vary as regards how many *Vulcans* there are. Recent estimates place the total number between 48 and 56.[8] Britain also operates five squadrons of *Buccaneer* strike aircraft which are based both in Britain and in West Germany. The total number of *Buccaneers* is between 56 and 60.[9] Both the *Vulcans* and the *Buccaneers* are 'nuclear-capable', but, according to one recent study, 'precisely how many of these British aircraft . . . are today assigned to nuclear weapon delivery apparently is not publicly known'.[10] Finally, there are 72 nuclear-capable *Jaguars* which are divided into four squadrons and are stationed in Britain and in West Germany.

Among Britain's purely 'tactical' nuclear weapons are nuclear depth charges carried by British maritime helicopters stationed both on shore and on board ships. These are for use in anti-submarine warfare (ASW). Nuclear depth charges are also carried by Britain's 27 *Nimrod* maritime patrol aircraft. The *Nimrod* bombs are, however, controlled by what is known as the 'double-key' system. This is a system whereby nuclear weapons are kept under the joint control of two nations — in this case the United States and Great Britain — in a way which is meant to ensure that neither can use the weapons without the consent of the other. This is accomplished by placing the weapons system — less the warheads — in the possession of the British, while allowing the Americans to retain control over the warheads. If ever both sides agree that it is necessary to use the weapons, the Americans will unlock the trigger mechanisms inside the warheads and turn the warheads over to the British.[11]

The two other types of tactical nuclear weapon operated by British forces are also under the double-key system. One of these is the *Lance* short-range ballistic missile (SRBM). The British Army on the Rhine (BAOR) has 264 *Lance* SRBMs, for which there are 20 reloadable launchers. The other is the US-made self-propelled howitzer, which is also operated by the BAOR. The howitzers come in two sizes (the M-109 155mm and the M-110 203mm) and are 'dual-capable' (that is, capable of firing either conventional or nuclear shells).[12]

The third category of weapons which I cited earlier is the category of American 'forward-based' weapons. As the name implies, these are not British weapons, but since they are stationed in Britain they are clearly relevant to our inquiry. It is up to the British Government whether to allow these weapons to remain in Britain or to order them to be removed. (Occasionally when I refer to 'British nuclear weapons', I shall be including American forward-based systems.)

The major forward-based nuclear weapons systems in Britain are the 170 F-111 bombers stationed at Lakenheath and Upper Heyford. But more important even than the weapons are the numerous strategic support facilities which the US maintains throughout Great Britain. These are military facilities which contribute to America's ability to fight a nuclear war, whether it be a European war or a strategic war (that is, a war involving the territories of the superpowers). A recent report in the *New Statesman* has revealed just how extensive these facilities are:

> In Britain, the US forces have at least 21 airbases used [by] or reserved for them, 9 transportation terminals, 17 weapon dumps and stores, 7 nuclear weapons stores, 38 communications facilities, 10 intelligence bases, and 3 radar and sonar surveillance sites. Of these, the majority clearly contribute at least as much to strategic global 'US only' options as to the options for defending Europe.[13]

Among the most important of these facilities are the submarine tracking station at Brawdy in South Wales, the base for American *Polaris* and *Poseidon* submarines at Holy Loch, and the Ballistic Missile Early Warning Station at Fylingdales in the Yorkshire Moors. Air bases in Britain also provide facilities for 'visiting' US B-52 strategic bombers.

Other American nuclear weapons systems which, though not visibly linked with Great Britain, may be relevant to this inquiry are the 40 to 45 *Poseidon* SLBMs assigned to NATO and the bombers on American aircraft carriers patrolling European waters.

This inventory of British nuclear weapons would not be complete without mention being made of the weapons which

Britain is scheduled to acquire in the future. These include the controversial *Trident* and cruise missiles, as well as the less well-known *Tornado* bombers.

On 15 July 1980 the Government announced their decision to purchase *Trident* SLBMs from the US. As in the case of *Polaris*, for which *Trident* is intended as a replacement, the missiles will be fitted with British warheads, and will be carried on board four British-built submarines. Again there will be 16 missiles per submarine, with each missile carrying multiple warheads. The *Trident* warheads will, however, be 'independently targetable', which means that they are designed to separate from the body of the missile and attack different targets spread over a very wide area. (These are what are known as 'multiple independently-targetable re-entry vehicles', or 'MIRVs'.) Since each missile will carry up to eight warheads, the new *Trident* force will, in the words of Lord Hill-Norton, 'more than double the striking power of our [present] strategic nuclear deterrent'.[14] The *Trident* force, if and when it is eventually deployed, will enjoy the same degree of independence as *Polaris* (or perhaps one should say, following one recent writer, that 'it [will] be no more independent than is *Polaris*'[15]).

The Government have also agreed to accept the stationing of 160 *Tomahawk* ground-launched cruise missiles (GLCMs) on British soil as part of the NATO programme for the 'modernization' of its theatre nuclear forces. These cruise missiles are pilotless aircraft designed to fly at an altitude of less than 150 feet at the subsonic speed of 500 miles per hour. They are intended to fly at low altitudes in order to avoid detection by enemy radar (though at present there is some doubt about whether 150 feet is low enough to avoid radar detection,[16] and about whether cruise missiles are actually capable of manoeuvring properly at such a low altitude). Cruise missiles use an extremely sophisticated form of navigation called 'terrain contour matching' which enables them to strike their targets with very great accuracy. As it flies the cruise missile surveys the terrain with radar and then compares the readings it takes with a map of the terrain stored in the memory bank of an on-board computer. By making constant corrections in the light of these comparisons the cruise missile can follow its pre-programmed flight path with great precision.

At present the plan is to base 96 cruise missiles at Greenham Common in Berkshire by the end of 1983, and to base a further 64 at Molesworth in Cambridgeshire in 1988. They will be mounted four apiece on the backs of lorries, and thus can be dispersed throughout the countryside in times of crisis. They will be entirely under American control. They are, nevertheless, normally classified as NATO weapons rather than American forward-based weapons. Why they are not referred to as American forward-based weapons is rather obscure, unless it is to foster the illusion among Europeans that the European allies will maintain some degree of control over them.

While both *Trident* and cruise missiles have been the subjects of considerable controversy, the decision to purchase 385 nuclear-capable *Tornado* fighter-bombers has been allowed to pass almost unnoticed. This is curious since, at £5,000 million, they will cost almost as much as *Trident*. The RAF must be holding its breath, hoping that these can be sneaked into service without too much fuss. They are intended as replacements for the *Vulcans* and for three of the squadrons of *Buccaneers*.

This concludes my survey of the weapons with which this book will be concerned. British defence policy could in principle be based on having any combination of these various types of nuclear weapon, including having all or none. As was mentioned earlier, different arguments will support different policies.

There is some confusion about which policy should be characterized as 'unilateral nuclear disarmament' for Britain. This is a term which regularly turns up in discussions about nuclear weapons, and it is therefore worth trying to determine what is or should be meant by it. Strictly speaking, to give up any one of the weapons systems mentioned above without requiring that this be accompanied by a parallel move on the part of Britain's adversaries, or compensated for by the acquisition of a nuclear replacement, would be an act of unilateral nuclear disarmament. Yet it is not uncommon to find people who claim to be in favour of unconditionally withdrawing certain types of nuclear weapon, and at the same time to be opposed to unilateral nuclear disarmament. This suggests that the term 'unilateral nuclear disarmament' should be reserved for relatively complete nuclear disarmament. I say 'relatively' complete because I can imagine someone claiming that to abandon all of the weapons owned by Britain, while allowing American forward-based systems to stay, would nevertheless be for Britain an act of unilateral disarmament.

Before proceeding to the examination of the arguments, I shall provide a brief summary of the contents of the remainder of the book. In Chapter II I shall look at the arguments in favour of Britain's having nuclear weapons. I shall begin with the strategic arguments, which are, unfortunately, the most difficult. If at first this chapter seems rather heavy going, it will lighten up when I come to consider the political arguments. Next, in Chapter III, I shall turn to the arguments for abandoning some or all of Britain's nuclear weapons. What the reader will find in this survey of the arguments is that I shall point out the strengths and weaknesses on both sides. In the concluding chapter I shall weigh up the arguments in order to arrive at a conclusion as to whether or not Britain should continue to have nuclear weapons. In the end I shall come down on the side of the nuclear disarmers, though perhaps not in a way that all of them will find attractive, and not without conceding the merits of the opposing point of view.

II

ARGUMENTS FOR THE RETENTION OF NUCLEAR WEAPONS

In this chapter I propose to examine a number of arguments for keeping some or all of Britain's nuclear weapons, or for acquiring new nuclear weapons, such as *Trident* or cruise missiles. For each argument I shall try to show to which types of nuclear weapon it applies.

Most of the arguments I shall consider in this section are based on the assumption that Britain and indeed all of the countries of Western Europe are faced with a serious military threat from the Soviet Union and its Warsaw Pact allies. It is assumed that the Soviet Union is an expansionist power seeking world domination. In particular, it is assumed that, if we let our guard down, the Soviet Union might then attempt to invade and colonize Western Europe.

Since many of the arguments in favour of having nuclear weapons depend on this perception of Soviet intentions, one way of attacking them would be simply to reject the view that the Russians have or might come to have aggressive designs on Western Europe. To my mind, however, this would be too swift a victory. It would be, in many cases, an unpersuasive way of arguing with defenders of nuclear weapons, whose views about the nature of the Soviet leadership and their intentions are unlikely to be significantly changed by a show of the evidence on the other side. This may seem a cynical thing to say, but I think it would be unrealistic to suppose that mistrust of a traditional enemy is likely to be dispelled by the force of rational argument.

It seems preferable, therefore, to address these arguments on their own terms by granting the assumption that there is a significant Soviet threat. Later, after discussing these arguments, I shall return to the question of the Soviet threat, and shall then examine the grounds for thinking that such a threat exists.

The Second Centre Argument and the Last Resort Deterrent Argument

In this section I shall consider two arguments together. The reason for considering them together is that they raise identical questions.

The first of these I shall refer to as the 'second centre argument'.[1] It is the argument most frequently heard in government circles, both now and in the past. It holds that deterrence is enhanced by having in Britain a second centre of nuclear decision-making within the Alliance; for the presence of an additional finger on the nuclear trigger introduces an additional source of fear in the Soviet mind, thereby increasing Soviet reluctance to launch an attack against Western Europe.[2] (Government spokesmen usually refrain from claiming that having the separate centre of decision-making actually increases the probability that a Soviet attack on Western Europe would provoke nuclear retaliation. This would imply that they believed that the Americans might be unwilling to respond to a Soviet attack on Europe by retaliating with nuclear weapons, and members of the government are understandably anxious to avoid giving the impression that they believe this.)

Since this argument depends for its force on the British being able to use nuclear weapons independently, all that it supports is the maintenance by Britain of an independent nuclear capacity. It cannot be used to justify the possession of NATO weapons under the double-key system, or the stationing of American forward-based systems in Britain.

The uncertainty which the second centre of decision is supposed to create in the Soviet mind must concern the possibility that the British would use their nuclear weapons against the Soviet Union at a time when the Americans would be unwilling to use theirs. Thus the force of the argument depends not only on Britain's *ability* to use nuclear weapons independently, but also on Britain's *willingness* to do so. To be more exact, it depends on the supposition that the Russians will *believe* that the British would be willing to use nuclear weapons independently. If Britain's threat to use nuclear weapons independently is not found credible by the Russians, then British independent weapons will not enhance deterrence in the way that the second centre argument claims they will.

There is another argument which also hangs on the assumption that the threat of British independent use of nuclear weapons is plausible. This is the argument that British independent nuclear weapons provide a ' "last resort" national deterrent'[3] to be used if ever Britain must again 'stand alone'. Of course, the Americans are committed to using their nuclear weapons in defence of Britain, but the independent deterrent provides insurance against the possibility that the Americans might in the end fail to honour that commitment. (As I mentioned above, Government spokesmen are reluctant to concede that the Americans might not honour their obligations. This is why one finds the second centre argument but not the last resort deterrent argument cited in official publications. These two arguments are substantially the same argument. The only real difference is that, while the second centre argument holds that the second centre is valuable because the *Russians* might believe that the US would not come to our defence, the last resort deterrent argument holds that the second centre is valuable because *we* believe that the Americans might not come to our defence.)

It is crucial for both of these arguments that the Russians can be expected to believe that, given sufficient provocation, the British would fire their weapons independently. Therefore, in order to determine whether or not the second centre and last resort deterrent arguments are sound, we need to know how credible the threat of independent use actually is.

In a debate in the House of Lords late in 1979, Lord Carver, the former Defence Chief of Staff, made the following statement:

I have never heard or read a scenario which I would consider to be realistic in which it could be considered to be right or reasonable for the Prime Minister or Government of this country to order the firing of our independent strategic force at a time when the Americans were not prepared to fire theirs — certainly not before Russian nuclear weapons had landed in this country. And, again, if they had already landed, would it be right and reasonable? All it would do would be to invite further retaliation.[4]

For the most part this seems right. I shall later suggest that there is one clear exception, and another possible exception to Lord Carver's claim. For the moment, however, I shall try to show the respects in which he is right. The main point is that Britain's independent nuclear force is not credible as a direct deterrent to the one threat it is primarily intended to deter — namely, a Soviet invasion of Western Europe.

It should be remembered that the options provided by Britain's independent nuclear weapons are severely limited. The choice for Britain would seem to be between firing a warning shot (aimed, presumably, against a military target inside Soviet or Warsaw Pact territory), in the hope that this would dissuade the Russians from persisting in their aggressive action, and striking a Soviet city. Let us consider these two options, first on the assumption that Soviet missiles have already landed in Britain.

The main reason which the Russians would have for attacking Britain with nuclear weapons in the course of an invasion of Western Europe would be to destroy as many of the nuclear weapons stationed in Britain as possible. This would be a mere matter of prudence, since it would prevent these weapons from being used against the Russians. Obviously, a primary target of the Soviet strike would be the *Polaris* submarines which are resting vulnerably in port. Britain's retaliatory capacity resides almost solely in the *Polaris* force. But usually there is only one *Polaris* submarine out at sea at any given time. At other times there are at most only two. This is because nuclear submarines must spend a lot of their time in port being serviced. But this means that, if Soviet missiles had landed in Britain, they would probably have destroyed two or possibly three of Britain's four submarines.

Suppose that Britain is left with only one boat. To fire a warning shot from this boat would be irrational, for it would serve to reveal to the Russians the location of the submarine, thereby enabling them to destroy it. And, as Lord Carver notes, it would also invite retaliation, which Britain, now effectively disarmed, would be unable to deter. And to fire against one or more Soviet cities would be even more irrational: it would be suicidal. So with deterrence having already failed, a sane British leader in this situation would not retaliate.

Suppose, on the other hand, that we make the more optimistic assumption that Britain has more than one submarine at sea. It is entirely possible that two boats could be at sea, and, if Britain had sufficient warning that war seemed likely, it is conceivable that extraordinary measures could have been taken in order to place three boats on patrol. Would this make it more reasonable for Britain to fire a warning shot, or to attack a Soviet city?

First, it seems to me highly unlikely that, by firing a warning shot, Britain would be able to persuade the Russians simply to turn around and go home. Remember that we are supposing that the Americans have not yet used nuclear weapons. The Russians might seize the opportunity provided by the warning shot to demonstrate to the Americans their determination to meet any attack with retaliation. By retaliating against Britain, the Russians might hope to send a signal to the Americans which would help to deter the Americans from using their nuclear weapons.

A second consideration is that, by striking only military targets, the Russians would have signalled their conditional intention not to attack British cities. (Of course, millions of British civilians would be killed during a large-scale counter-force strike — that is, a strike against military targets — but the Russians would have an incentive to avoid direct strikes against British cities.[5]) But there would have been an implicit threat — or even an explicit one — to respond to any British retaliation by attacking British cities. So, in firing a retaliatory warning shot, Britain would not only reveal the location of one of its submarines, thereby weakening its deterrent against further attacks, but it would also risk drawing fire on

British cities.

It is conceivable that, if the warning shot were directed against a relatively unimportant target, the Russians would not return fire — at least not against British cities. But a warning shot of this sort would serve no purpose. It would not be sufficient to deter the Russians, who would regard the destruction of, say, a relatively minor military installation as an acceptable price to pay for the destruction of a large number of British nuclear weapons and American forward-based systems. They would also be happy to learn of the whereabouts of the British submarine which had fired the shot.

To respond to the Soviet strike against Britain's nuclear weapons by blowing up a Russian city would be even more unreasonable. It would almost inevitably bring retaliation against one or more British cities. At a time when there would be no immediate threat to British cities, it would be foolish to create one.

So it would seem that, even if the Russians had already conducted a counterforce strike, it would not be reasonable for Britain to use its missiles independently. And it would be even less reasonable for Britain to fire if Soviet missiles had not already landed. Suppose that Britain has only one boat at sea. (The others might have been destroyed while at sea by Soviet hunter-killer submarines.) Again, it would be madness to fire a warning shot or attack a city, since this would only provoke retaliation and allow Britain to be disarmed. And even if two or three boats were at sea, it would still be imprudent to fire. A warning shot might provide the Russians with a pretext for conducting a counterforce strike against Britain, and an attack on a Russian city would provoke attacks on British cities. It would seem, therefore, that it would be unreasonable for Britain to use its retaliatory nuclear weapons independently simply in the event of a Soviet invasion of Western Europe.

In general, the credibility of a threat to retaliate depends on how reasonable it would be for the threatener to carry out the retaliation. Thus, a country which has invulnerable nuclear forces can with complete plausibility threaten to retaliate in response to a *massive* nuclear attack. This is because retaliation after an all-out attack would not be irrational from a self-interested point of view. The country which had been attacked would have little or nothing else to lose.

Earlier I mentioned that there is one clear exception to Lord Carver's claim that it would never be reasonable to use nuclear weapons independently. This exception has been suggested in the previous paragraph. If Britain had already been bombed so heavily that it had little else to fear from the Russians, then it would not be irrational from a self-interested point of view for Britain to retaliate. Indeed, it would not be irrational for it to retaliate using its every remaining weapon. And, since it would not be irrational to retaliate in these circumstances, the threat to do so is quite credible. British independent nuclear weapons are therefore a credible deterrent against an all-out nuclear attack on Britain.

If the Russians wanted to destroy Britain totally, then it seems to me that it would be an undeniable advantage for Britain to have an independent nuclear force capable of retaliating against the Soviet Union. Analogously, if those groups whose avowed aim is the total destruction of the population of Israel were to acquire nuclear weapons, then I would think it better for Israel also to have nuclear weapons. But it is difficult to see what reason the Russians could ever have for wanting to destroy Britain totally. Even if Britain were bristling with nuclear weapons, and posed a grave threat to Russian security, the Russians would have a reason only for wanting to disarm Britain, not to destroy its cities. And if Britain had no nuclear weapons, and posed no threat to the Soviet Union, then it would be even more difficult to imagine a plausible situation in which the Russians would have a reason for wanting to destroy Britain totally. The most realistic scenario I can think of in which the Russians would have a reason for blowing up all of Britain would be if, in a time of war, the Russians wanted to deliver a dramatic warning to the Americans. They might then use the destruction of Britain as a grim demonstration of what would happen to the US if it were to attack the Soviet Union. Even this, however, is pretty unrealistic. (It will perhaps be said that they might wish to destroy Britain out of sheer unmotivated malice. This is not only wildly implausible, but it would also be unrewarding: for the amount of fallout it would bring down upon the Soviet Union itself would not be negligible.) In short, though having independent nuclear weapons is a credible deterrent against an all-out nuclear attack, the ability to deter an all-out nuclear attack is far from being an urgent defence requirement.

In the scenarios we have considered, it seems that it would be unreasonable for Britain to fire against the Soviet Union. This is because Britain would have a great deal to lose by firing, and would have little chance of gaining anything by doing so. Equally importantly, Britain would have a great deal more to lose than would the Soviet Union. The Russians are, moreover, clearly aware that there is this asymmetry. They once responded to a statement of British nuclear weapons policy by observing that 'people in glass houses shouldn't throw stones'.[6] But if it would be unreasonable for Britain to use its nuclear weapons independently in these circumstances, and if the Russians know this, then the threat to use them independently will be only doubtfully credible, and will be unlikely to serve the purpose of deterrence.

This conclusion is reinforced by a comparison with the reasoning of certain American strategic theorists. These theorists are very worried about what they refer to as the '*Minutemen* vulnerability problem'.[7] The problem as they perceive it is that America's *Minutemen* force — the land-based intercontinental ballistic missiles (ICBMs) — will soon be perilously vulnerable to a 'disarming first strike' by the Soviet Union. The reason that this is so deeply worrying to them is as follows. Suppose that the Russians launch a surprise first strike against American ICBMs. Because many Russian missiles are 'MIRVed' — that is, because the Russian missiles each carry a number of warheads, each of which can strike a different target — the number of missiles which the Russians would have to use in conducting the strike would be far fewer than the number of American missiles they could hope to destroy. For example, they might hope to destroy four or five American missiles for each missile they fire. They would, of course, fail to destroy a certain number of American ICBMs, and the Americans would presumably still have a number of submarines and bombers left; but at the end of the day the Russians would have considerably more striking power than the Americans.

What should the Americans do? They know that if they were to expend most of their remaining firepower against Soviet cities it would provoke retaliation on a scale which would destroy the US forever. Since the great majority of the American people would have survived the initial counter-force strike, the American leaders will be anxious to preserve the remaining population from harm. They might, therefore, contemplate using most of their remaining nuclear weapons to destroy as many Soviet weapons as possible, thereby limiting the amount of further damage the Russians could do. At the same time they could hold some weapons in reserve in order to threaten Soviet cities, hoping thereby to deter Soviet strikes against American cities.

But, as American planners recognize, this second option would also be hopeless. Anticipating the possibility of an American response aimed at destroying Soviet forces, the Russians would be prepared to launch some of their remaining forces as soon as they were alerted of an approaching American attack. This means that many of the American missiles would end up striking empty missile silos, while Russian missiles would be on their way towards certain remaining military targets in the US and probably one or two American cities. (The Russians too would presumably spare most American cities, holding them hostage in order to deter further American retaliation.)

The Americans, then, would be faced with the stark choice between surrender and annihilation. This is why they are so worried about the possibility of a Soviet first strike. Notice, however, that they would not be worried if they thought that the Russians confidently believed that the American leaders would prefer annihilation to surrender. If the Russians believed this, they would not launch a first strike. The Americans know, however, that they cannot expect the Russians to have this belief. They know that the Russians recognize that surrender would be the more reasonable course, and might therefore be tempted by the prospect of success to launch a first strike.

The moral of this story should be obvious. Britain at the peak of readiness, with three or even four boats at sea, would be *far* weaker and more vulnerable than the US would be even after absorbing a 'disarming' first strike. If the Russians could reasonably expect that the US would not in these circumstances retaliate (and American planners assume that the Russians could expect this), then they could even more reasonably expect that Britain would not retaliate. And insofar as they have good reason to believe that Britain would not retaliate, they will to that extent not be deterred by the threat of retaliation.

What the foregoing argument shows, if it is sound, is that people who defend the credibility of Britain's threat to use nuclear weapons independently are relying on far more optimistic assumptions about what the Russians can be expected to believe than are relied on by American military planners. We are entitled to ask why these people feel justified in making these more optimistic assumptions.

There is a reply to this challenge. This reply accepts the claim that the British threat to retaliate is no more credible than the American threat to retaliate after suffering a first strike. But it contends that there is this difference: a threat which is only doubtfully credible may serve to deter an aggressor if the prize he seeks is small, but may not deter him if the prize he seeks is more important to him. Clearly the domination of Britain would be a much smaller prize to the Russians than would be the domination of the US. So it is conceivable that the British threat will deter the Russians, while the American threat would not, even if the British threat is no more credible than the American threat would be.

This reply, while interesting, ignores two important facts. The first of these is that it is highly unlikely that the Soviet Union would ever take aggressive action against Britain alone. If the Russians ever attempt to invade Britain, it will be in the course of a larger invasion of all of Western Europe. Therefore, in risking retaliation from the British, the Russians would be seeking a more valuable prize than simply the conquest of Britain: they would be seeking the conquest of Europe. (This fact is partly — though only partly — counterbalanced by the fact that, in invading Europe, the Russians would also risk retaliation from France.) Second, while the gains to be derived from the domination of the US would be greater than those to be derived from the domination of Britain or Western Europe, the Russians would also stand to lose more if the Americans were to retaliate than they would if the British were to retaliate. The fact that America would be a bigger prize does not, therefore, undermine my argument. Western Europe would not be of negligible value, and in any case the fact that the prize would be bigger is at least partly made up for by the fact that the risks involved in going for the bigger prize would be greater.

Thus far I have argued that, in order to deter a Soviet invasion of Western Europe, the British threat to use nuclear weapons independently in the event of an invasion must be credible to the Russians — which it is probably not. I shall now suggest that there is a further problem, which is that the threat of independent use by the British might even be counterproductive. This problem arises from the possibility that the Americans may be more ready than the Russians to believe that the British would use nuclear weapons independently.

Suppose that the Russians have begun an invasion of Western Europe. If the Americans believe that the British would be willing to fire their weapons independently, then they may be tempted to hold back their own weapons in the expectation that the British will fire first. There are several reasons why the Americans might want the first shots to be fired by the British. An initial British salvo might provide the Americans with a valuable probe of Soviet intentions, while minimizing the risk of Soviet retaliation against the American homeland. The Americans might also hope that the war could be brought to a close without their ever having to be drawn into it. And, finally, if the British were to fire first, this would allow the Americans to avoid the opprobrium which would attach to the first use of nuclear weapons. In short, the possibility of British independent use provides the US with a reason for holding back.

The British must therefore hope that the Russians, but not the Americans, will be impressed by their threat to use nuclear weapons independently. And in fact it is not unlikely that, given their different perspectives, the Russians and the Americans will have divergent perceptions of British intentions. But it is entirely possible that things could work the wrong way round. If so, then the British threat would not deter the Russians, but it might present the US and Britain with a formidable coordination problem: since each would prefer the other to fire first, each might refrain from firing in the hope that the other *will* fire first. This problem would be particularly acute if the Russians could succeed in damaging or destroying communications links between command posts in the US and Britain.

Now, in itself this reluctance on the part of each country to initiate a nuclear exchange might be highly desirable. What should be worrying for proponents of the second centre argument is that the possibility of confusion and indecision arising from the existence of separate centres of decision might be seen by the Russians as decreasing the likelihood that an invasion would be met by retaliation. This would, of course, have the effect of weakening deterrence — the opposite effect from that which the separate centre is supposed to have.

The last resort deterrent argument faces the same problem. If the Americans believe that Britain is ready and willing to stand alone, they may be quite happy to let Britain do just that. In this case, having the insurance may be instrumental in bringing about the crisis which Britain is concerned to insure against. In short, both the second centre argument and the last resort deterrent argument can cut both ways, given different assumptions as to how the threat of independent use is likely to be perceived.

The foregoing argument is admittedly not very powerful if I am right in my main claim that the threat of independent use by the British in the event of a Soviet invasion is *clearly* not credible. This claim has been endorsed not only by Lord Carver, but also by Robert McNamara, the former American Secretary of Defence. Several of the points for which I have argued in detail in support of this claim were stated in summary fashion by McNamara as far back as 1962. In his famous Ann Arbor speech, he stated that relatively weak nuclear forces with enemy cities as their targets are not likely to be sufficient to perform even the function of deterrence. If they are small, and perhaps vulnerable on the ground or in the air, or inaccurate, a major antagonist can take a variety of measures to counter them. Indeed, if a major antagonist came to believe there was a substantial likelihood of it being used independently, this force would be inviting a 'pre-emptive' first strike against it. In the event of war, the use of such a force against cities of a major nuclear power would be tanta-mount to suicide, while its employment against significant military targets would have a negligible effect on the outcome of the conflict. . . . In short then, limited nuclear capabilities, operating independently, are dangerous, expensive, prone to obsolescence and lacking in credibility as a deterrent.[8]

In this passage, McNamara concedes that it is not impos-sible that a 'major nuclear power' (the Soviet Union) would believe that a minor nuclear power (Britain) would be willing to use nuclear weapons independently. I do not wish to deny this. My point is only that in most instances it is sufficiently unlikely that the major power would believe this to make it unwise for the minor power to rely for its defence on the threat of using nuclear weapons independently.

McNamara's remarks suggest a further reason for thinking that British independent weapons are of doubtful value as a deterrent. This is that, even if Britain were clearly willing to use the weapons, it is possible that the weapons themselves might be rendered largely ineffective. There are two ways in which the Russians might be able to reduce the effectiveness of the British forces. One is to develop more effective means of destroying them preemptively. The other is to develop more adequate defences against them. Both of these measures are increasingly possible in the case of a relatively small nuclear force.

It is true, of course, that at present the effectiveness of Britain's independent nuclear force is not in doubt. Almost all of Britain's retaliatory capability is now and will continue to be invested in a force of submarine-launched ballistic missiles. Of the various bases for nuclear weapons, submarines are the least vulnerable to preemptive attack. Moreover, there are at present no adequate means of defending against an attack by ballistic missiles, and the deployment of large-scale ballistic missile defence systems (ABMs) is in any case banned by the SALT I agreement. (Under this agreement, each side is permitted a single ABM site. Thus the Russians have a relatively primitive ABM network set up around Moscow.)

But, while the effectiveness of the independent force seems guaranteed for the short term, there is nevertheless reason for doubting whether this guarantee can extend to the long term as well. The US has recently made dramatic advances in anti-submarine warfare (ASW) technology, and there is every reason to expect further advances in the future.[9] The Soviet Union is presently lagging behind, but it is certainly not for lack of will. The fear is that, by the time that the *Trident* force can be ready for deployment, ASW techniques will be perfected to such a degree that the new force will then be effectively obsolete — that is, before it even enters into service.

The possibility that *Trident* will be vulnerable to preemption has been considered by Lord Hill-Norton, whose response is simply to note that 'any breakthrough that helps enemy underwater hunter-killers to stalk our *Trident* vessels will also enable our submarines to knock out theirs'.[10] This reply is hardly reassuring. The deterrent value of a small nuclear force depends at the very minimum on its being invulnerable to preemption. It is difficult to see what comfort could be derived from the knowledge that, even if one's own retaliatory forces could be destroyed before they could be used, one would still be able to attack a few of the other side's submarines. (It is also curious that Hill-Norton assumes that the breakthrough would be achieved simultaneously by both sides.)

A more persuasive response to the potential problem of *Trident* vulnerability might be constructed on the basis of the assumption that the Russians will be unable to tell whether the submarine they are tracking is a British *Trident* or an American *Trident*. It is not clear whether this assumption will turn out to be true. At present it is true that the

Russians cannot distinguish between a British and an American *Polaris* submarine. If this ambiguity still exists when the *Trident* force enters service it could serve to enhance the 'survivability' of the British force. The reason is as follows. Suppose that the Soviet Union is embarked upon an invasion of Western Europe and that, while the US seems anxious to avoid getting involved, Britain has threatened to attack Soviet territory with nuclear weapons. Suppose further that the Russians are tracking a number of *Trident* submarines. They would presumably want to destroy the British ones preemptively, but, if they cannot tell which are the British and which are the American, then they will presumably refrain from attacking any of them. For, to destroy an American submarine by accident would carry with it a high risk of drawing the US into the conflict. If, therefore, the British *Trident* force will be indistinguishable from the American, this will significantly reduce the vulnerability of Britain's retaliatory capability in cases in which Britain may have to act independently. (Having submarines indistinguishable from American ones may also prove to be a liability. I shall return to this in the second section of this chapter.)

There are, however, reasons for doubting whether the British *Tridents* will be able to enjoy the benefits of anonymity. One is that, since the British submarines will be built in the UK, they may differ in design from those built in and operated by the US. Another is that it may eventually be possible for the Russians to recognize or identify individual submarines. It is, in fact, rumoured that the Americans already have this capability to some extent. If advances in ASW make this sort of detection possible, then the British *Trident* force will be highly vulnerable to preemptive attack.

The second threat to the continued viability of the British independent nuclear force is that the Russians may eventually develop systems adequate to defend against a relatively small-scale ballistic missile attack with a high degree of success. Both the US and the Soviet Union are presently engaged in intensive research on new types of ABM systems involving the use of lasers and charged particle-beam weapons. In the US, research is being conducted at such a feverish pace that the programme has been compared, perhaps with some exaggeration, to the Manhattan Project which produced the first atomic bomb in 1945.[11] The propaganda campaign in favour of a new ABM system is also becoming aggressive. Recently, General Daniel Graham, a campaign advisor to Reagan on military affairs, said before a group of defence experts in Washington that 'we [the US] must seize lunar space for the United States. If we do, we will restore US superiority over the Soviet Union, not parity.'[12] The fact that ABM systems are banned under SALT I may be of little significance. The new Reagan administration's defence budget has set aside funds for the development of new ABM systems, and the current Defense Secretary, Mr Caspar Weinberger, has suggested that the ABM treaty may not be renewed when it comes up for review in 1982. The administration even has plans for the testing of a new ABM system under operational conditions in 1982.[13] Of course, if the US abrogates or violates the ABM ban under SALT I, the Soviet Union will then cease to be bound by it. And, if the Soviet Union were to erect a network of ABM systems geared to defend against a large-scale attack by US missiles, this would provide ample protection against even the most massive attack that could be mounted using Britain's much smaller missile force.

It is at present difficult to assess whether and to what extent the effectiveness of *Trident* is likely to be impaired by future developments in ASW or ABM technology. Dramatic breakthroughs in these areas have been predicted in the past, but these predictions have thus far proved unfounded. This is, however, rather weak evidence for the view that breakthroughs are unlikely to occur.

The main conclusion of this section is that Britain's threat to use nuclear weapons independently against the Soviet Union in the event of an invasion of Europe is lacking in credibility. This is partly because future developments in ASW and ABM technology may prevent Britain from being *able* to carry out the threat of retaliation, but it is mainly because the Russians are likely to believe that the constraints of rationality will prevent Britain from being *willing* to carry out the threat.[14] But a threat which is only doubtfully credible is unlikely to serve the purpose of deterrence. Since the second centre and last resort deterrent arguments depend on the assumption that the threat of independent use is credible, much of their force is presumably undermined by the foregoing criticisms. If so, this is an important result, since these arguments constitute two of the main military or strategic rationales for the possession of independent nuclear weapons.

The Trigger Argument

Having perceived the implausibility of a British threat to engage in a nuclear contest with the Soviet Union in the event of an invasion of Western Europe, certain writers have suggested that the second centre argument, rather than collapsing altogether, collapses into a different, though closely related argument. The idea is that Britain might have another aim in using nuclear weapons independently than simply to fight the Russians single-handedly. This other aim would be to serve as a catalyst for engaging the American nuclear forces. By using nuclear weapons itself, Britain might be able to force the Americans to use nuclear weapons also. (I shall shortly consider two ways in which this might be done.)

If Britain has the ability to force the Americans to use nuclear weapons, this will reinforce deterrence in Europe in the following way. The Russians will be deterred from invading Western Europe if they feel confident that this would lead to a nuclear war with the US. But they may feel that the US would be reluctant to risk annihilation by going to war for the sake of Europe. But, if Britain holds the key to escalation, and can force the Americans to become involved, this will clearly strengthen the guarantee of American involvement. For Britain's leaders might feel that it would be worth the risk of starting a global war by bringing the Americans into the conflict, if by bringing them in the British might hope to halt the invasion. Finally, if Britain's using nuclear weapons independently *for these purposes* could be considered rational, then the threat to use them will be credible. If it is credible, then it will strengthen deterrence.

This argument has, for obvious reasons, been referred to as the 'trigger argument'. There are, in fact, two versions of the argument. Only one of these versions is an extension of the second centre argument. This is the argument which I have just summarized. It holds that *independent* weapons constitute the most reliable mechanism for triggering the involvement of American nuclear weapons. The other version holds that the 'trigger effect' is best accomplished by having in Britain (or Europe) NATO TNW under the double-key system and American forward-based systems. In short, the two versions of the argument support the possession of weapons from different categories.

Although each version of the trigger argument enjoys some measure of plausibility, I shall concentrate on the version which extends the second centre argument, largely because it is the more important of the two. But first I shall briefly discuss the other version.

Doubt has often been cast on the military utility of TNW. It has been claimed, for example, that TNW 'cannot be used successfully to keep a war at the border, nor can they be used to regain territory that has been lost to *blitzkrieg* assaults with conventional weapons'.[15] Most important, it is difficult to use them without exposing one's own troops to radioactive contamination and without destroying the territory which the weapons are intended to defend. (The neutron bomb constitutes an attempt to avoid these problems.) Thus, when West European governments first decided to accept the deployment of TNW on their soil, they did not, in the words of one commentator, 'really see TNW as battlefield weapons. For them, the point of TNW was to extend strategic deterrence from the USA to Western Europe and to gain as concrete a commitment as possible from the USA to link its own fate to that of West European States.'[16]

The idea, stated crudely, is that, if the US has its own nuclear weapons stationed in Europe, as well as nuclear weapons over which it shares control with European governments, this will make it very difficult for the US not to become involved in any war which might erupt in Europe. Since, moreover, these weapons are nuclear weapons, their presence increases the likelihood that any war in Europe involving the Soviet Union will escalate to the level of a strategic nuclear war between the superpowers. The implicit threat of escalation which these weapons pose is intended to deter the Russians from starting a war in Europe. This understanding of the function of TNW has remained widespread in Europe. As two American writers have observed, 'TNW generally continue to be regarded more politically for their "escalatory" potential than militarily for defensive or war-fighting purposes'.[17]

How successful can we expect NATO TNW to be in 'coupling' American and European security? One thing to bear in mind is that the weapons which this argument supports are ones over which Europeans have no independent control. The weapons are regarded as a trigger, but the British cannot pull the trigger without the consent of the Americans. Thus, as Dan Smith bluntly points out, the mere fact that these weapons are sitting in Europe provides no guarantee of American involvement: 'all the US president would have to do is refrain from releasing TNW to West European NATO forces'.[18] And even if the TNW were released, this in itself would not guarantee the involvement of the strategic forces based in the US. Whether or not the US strategic forces would have to become involved would presumably depend on what types of TNW the US would release. The use of the proposed cruise missiles against the Soviet Union would in all probability provoke a transatlantic exchange, for, as Michael Howard has pointed out, these missiles would be 'under American control, and any damage they inflict on the Soviet Union . . . will be seen as having been inflicted by Americans. The probability of retaliation against the United States would be no less than if the missiles had been based on American soil.'[19] But the release of other types of TNW — in particular those which would be incapable of striking inside the Soviet Union — would be less likely to provoke retaliation against the American homeland. Indeed, the selective release of weapons of this sort might allow the US simultaneously to claim that it had done its duty by the Europeans and to signal to the Soviet Union its desire to keep the war 'contained' in Europe. In other words, the release of weapons which could be used only in Europe might permit the superpowers to fight their war using Europe as the battle-field, while preserving their own territories as sanctuaries. (I shall consider the possibility of 'limited nuclear war in Europe' in more detail in Chapter III.)

Simply to raise doubts about the 'catalytic' role of NATO TNW is not, of course, to show that TNW play no useful role in the defence of Europe. The trigger argument in favour of TNW is only one argument, and I do not pretend to have refuted it decisively. Whether or not TNW are necessary or desirable for the defence of Europe is a very large and diffi-cult question. I shall have more to say about this later. For the moment I want to turn instead to the version of the trigger argument which is intended to support the possession of independent nuclear weapons.

This second version of the trigger argument can itself be subdivided into two separate arguments. These arguments both involve the claim that the trigger effect is best accom-plished by the *independent* use of British nuclear weapons. But each recommends the use of a different tactic. A further difference is that, while one of these tactics is better suited to triggering American involvement at the tactical level, the other is better suited to triggering the involvement of American forces at the strategic level. I shall examine each of these variants in turn.

The Tactic of Mere Escalation

One way in which Britain might hope to engage American forces would be simply to initiate the use of nuclear weapons at the level at which American involvement is desired. I shall refer to this as the 'tactic of mere escalation'. Here is an example of how it might work. Suppose that the Russians are engaged in a conventional invasion of Western Europe. It is certainly conceivable that the US might withhold TNW war-heads in an attempt to minimize the risk of a strategic exchange with the Soviet Union, with the consequence that Warsaw Pact conventional forces would begin to overwhelm their NATO counterparts. In these conditions, Britain might attempt to use a *Polaris* missile for tactical purposes — for example, to strike at Warsaw Pact reinforcements still in East

European territory. (It is open to question whether *Polaris* is accurate enough for such a purpose. On the other hand, there is no doubt that *Trident* will be sufficiently accurate. The problem with *Trident* is that, with eight independently targetable warheads on each missile, it provides far more than is needed for a single interdictory mission.) Britain could then expect that, once the nuclear threshold had been passed, the US would find it unconscionable to continue to withhold TNW.

To me it seems reasonable to assume that, after Britain had fired a nuclear weapon, the US would be more likely to release the TNW warheads. Their reason for holding back would be to keep the war from getting any closer to the strategic nuclear level. But, once the war had already escalated to the tactical nuclear level, the reason for their reluctance would have vanished. Britain's battlefield strike would, moreover, be considerably less likely to provoke nuclear retaliation against British cities than would an attack on Russian soil. It seems, therefore, that the threat to use nuclear weapons in this way has some measure of credibility. If so, then Britain's having this capacity should strengthen deterrence by strengthening the guarantee of American involvement.

While this argument seems fairly plausible, it is not wholly without problems. The risks attendant upon escalation would be enormous. There is, for example, the possibility that, during the interval when the American decision concerning the release of TNW was being taken and implemented, the Warsaw Pact would conduct swift preemptive strikes against NATO TNW delivery systems. The Warsaw Pact might earlier have been reluctant to make these strikes for fear of the consequences of crossing the nuclear threshold; but once the threshold had been violated they might have no further inhibitions to overcome. This problem would, of course, be avoided if the mere threat of independent use would be sufficient to prompt the release of TNW. But there is no guarantee that applying this sort of pressure would induce American compliance rather than simply reinforce American intractability.

There is, furthermore, the obvious possibility that escalation to the nuclear level would serve only to magnify NATO losses without significantly increasing the prospect of anything resembling victory. Remember that NATO would be fighting a defensive war on its own territory. Britain's West European allies might be less than grateful if Britain were to engineer an escalation in the war leading to an enormously higher degree of devastation in their territories.

The consideration of these possible consequences of escalation suggests that the range of occasions on which it would be rational to use the tactic of mere escalation is severely limited. It is difficult to imagine why anyone in the West would desire the escalation of a conventional war in Western Europe to the tactical nuclear level unless this would significantly enhance the prospect of a NATO victory. But if a NATO victory might be achieved by the introduction of TNW, then it is difficult to see why the US would refuse to introduce them. Of course, the European members of NATO would have a greater stake in the outcome of the war, and therefore might be more willing than the US to resort to desperate measures to avoid defeat; but they would also stand to lose more as a result of the use of TNW than the Americans would. So, on balance, there is no reason to suppose that the Americans would be more reluctant to use TNW than the West Europeans. But, if this is true, then it is highly unlikely that circumstances favourable to the use of the tactic of mere escalation will ever arise. The fact that independent weapons would enable Britain to engage in this tactic is, therefore, of limited significance.

It should be mentioned here that it would probably not be necessary to use Britain's independent force (that is, *Polaris* or *Trident*) in order to accomplish the aim of the tactic of mere escalation. As was mentioned earlier, there is a sense in which some of Britain's TNW are effectively independent. I know of no reason why these could not be used in desperation to attempt to trigger the release of NATO TNW. It would certainly be more rational to use, say, a nuclear bomber rather than *Polaris*. Not only would the *Polaris* missile be less accurate for a battlefield strike, but also the firing of the missile would give away the location of the submarine, making it easier for the Russians to destroy it.

I suggested earlier that the tactic of mere escalation is better suited to triggering the release of NATO TNW, thereby implying that it is not well suited to triggering the involvement of American strategic forces. I shall now suggest why this is so.

Again suppose that a war involving the Soviet Union is in progress in Europe, and that Britain wants to see the war escalate to the strategic level. (We can assume that the war is a conventional war or a tactical nuclear war, though the following scenario seems more plausible if we assume the latter.) Presumably Britain would desire escalation on the ground that, if the US were drawn in at the strategic level, the Russians might feel compelled to halt their attack and negotiate a settlement. The tactic of mere escalation would here require Britain to make a strategic strike against a target within the Soviet Union. It is, however, difficult to see how such a strike could be expected to provoke a transatlantic exchange. If the Russians were unaware that Britain's intention in firing the shot was only to effect the engagement of the US strategic forces, then their reaction would presumably be the same as in the case discussed earlier in which Britain fires a warning shot — that is, they would simply retaliate against Britain. If the Soviet perception of British intentions remains unchanged, then from the Soviet perspective this 'catalytic shot' would be indistinguishable from a warning shot.

Suppose, then, that Britain has previously indicated that its design in using nuclear weapons will be to trigger American involvement. Would it be reasonable to expect the Russians' response to be more restrained if they clearly understood that this was Britain's intention? It is important to notice that it is only if their response could be expected to be more restrained that it would be more reasonable for Britain to fire. And only if it would be more reasonable for Britain to fire would the threat to fire gain in credibility, thereby strengthening deterrence. But there seems to be no reason why this difference in British motivation would cause the Russians to temper their response. Indeed, since the Russians would be aware that the British strike had served as a desperate signal to the US, they might use the occasion to impress the US with their determination by responding swiftly and fiercely to the British attack. There is, moreover, the possibility that publicizing the intention of dragging the US into a nuclear war against its will would have the 'decoupling' effect of angering and alienating the American public. It is mainly for these reasons that it would be dangerously unwise to use the tactic of mere escalation to try to engage the American strategic forces.

The Tactic of Deception

A second way of triggering the involvement of American nuclear forces would be to deceive the Russians into thinking that they had been attacked by the US. This might in itself give the Russians pause and force them to reconsider their plans. Or it might simply bring 'retaliation' against the US, to which the US might then feel obliged to respond in kind. In any case the Russians would feel that the stakes had been raised dramatically.

This tactic, which I shall refer to as the 'tactic of deception', requires that Britain should be able to use nuclear weapons independently in such a way that the Russians would be uncertain as to the source of the attack. The necessary anonymity is provided by submarines. A shot fired from an untracked British submarine would be literally anonymous unless the British were to make a point of claiming responsibility. American leaders might deny over the hotline that the shot had been fired from an American boat, but this disavowal would not be fully trusted if neither Britain nor France had acknowledged responsibility. And even if the Russians were tracking the submarine at the time that it fired the shot, they presumably would not, as was mentioned earlier, be able to tell whether it was a British or an American boat. In short, the submarine force provides the British military with the capacity to strike the Soviet Union while masquerading as Americans.

Assuming that a war was already in progress in Europe (and again this could be either a conventional or a tactical nuclear war), the tactic of deception would, it seems, have a good chance of succeeding in engaging the American strategic forces. (This tactic would, however, be less useful as a trigger for the release of NATO TNW. An anonymous SLBM strike on the battlefield would not be perceived by the Russians as having come from an American boat. The Russians could assume that, if the Americans were unwilling even to release battlefield TNW, they would certainly not be firing SLBMs. Firing an anonymous SLBM on to the battlefield might succeed in triggering the release of TNW, but this would be simply because escalation had occurred, not because the Russians would be deceived.) In addition to having a good chance of success, the tactic of deception would carry with it a minimal risk of retaliation, since the Russians would not be expected to perceive the strike as British in origin. It follows from these two assumptions that the threat of independent use for purposes of deception should have considerable force.

The possibility of deception may therefore serve to restore plausibility to the second centre argument. If the possibility of deception makes the threat of independent use more credible, then the existence of the independent centre of decision may indeed cause the Russians to believe that an invasion would be more likely to meet with retaliation, and this would strengthen deterrence.

There is, however, a problem. In order for the threat of independent use to enjoy this enhanced credibility, the Russians must be made to believe that the British would be willing to practice deception. But any announcement of the British intention to deceive the Russians would presumably impair the ability of the British to carry out the deception. It is obvious, for example, that the British could not proclaim in a time of crisis that they were contemplating deceiving the Russians. This problem is only reduced, not eliminated, if the announcement is made during a period of stability, when the threat would not have reference to any particular occasion. Perhaps the only way of dealing with this problem would be to refrain from openly declaring the intention to deceive, and instead allow the threat to emerge by implication. In fact, this has already happened. There are now a sufficient number of references in western strategic literature to the possibility of deception that there can be no doubt that the Russians are well aware that there is an implicit threat of deception.[20]

While the previous objection to the tactic of deception appears to be rather weak, there is a second objection which is more damaging. Stated crudely, the idea is that, if the possibility of deception provides a way for the British to drag the Americans into a war, it equally provides a way for the Americans to drag the British into a war. If the British can masquerade as Americans, so can the Americans masquerade as Britons. This is a natural and inescapable corollary of trying to 'couple' American and European security via the possibility of deception. The possibility of deception also achieves the 'coupling' of American and European *in*security.

Of course, the American reasons for desiring anonymity would be different. The most obvious reason would be, not to gain British involvement in a war, or to draw retaliatory fire towards Britain, but simply to draw retaliatory fire away from the American homeland. What is perhaps less obvious is that the Russians themselves would have an interest in being able to direct their 'retaliation' at someone other than the US. Suppose that, during a crisis affecting Europe, the US were to launch a single anonymous SLBM against the Soviet Union. The Russians, while perhaps quite confident that the shot had been fired by the US, might nevertheless welcome the opportunity to feign ignorance and respond by attacking Great Britain, claiming that they have reason to suspect that the initial shot was fired by the British. This would allow the Russians to make a show of their strength and determination while at the same time allowing them to avoid the risks attendant upon attacking the US. It might also provide the occasion for transporting to the European theatre what might otherwise have been a largely strategic war. Clearly, the possibility of deception is a double-edged weapon.

I shall conclude this section by summarizing the results of this discussion of the various versions of the trigger argument. First, I argued that NATO TNW are of doubtful value as a trigger for the US strategic forces. The US President has the option of not releasing TNW warheads in the first place, and even if he were to release them he might do so in a selective way which could lead, not to strategic war, but to limited nuclear war in Europe. Second, I argued that, while the independent use of British nuclear weapons in accordance with the tactic of mere escalation would not work as a trigger for the American strategic forces, it would have a good chance of succeeding in triggering the release of NATO TNW. On the other hand, I concluded that it is highly unlikely that circumstances will ever arise in which it would be rational for Britain to use this tactic. Finally, I claimed that, while the tactic of deception might succeed in triggering the involvement of American strategic forces, the conditions which make the tactic possible might also work to Britain's disadvantage. The possibility of deception therefore provides reasons both for and against the possession of an independent submarine force. On the whole, it seems to me that the possibility of using nuclear weapons as a trigger for the American arsenal is so fraught with danger and uncertainty that such a possibility cannot be thought to provide a strong reason for possessing nuclear weapons.

The Free-Rider Argument

For reasons which will soon become evident, it is appropriate at this point to introduce a third argument which, if successful, would support the possession of nuclear weapons in all three categories. Put succinctly, the argument is that any renunciation of nuclear weapons by Great Britain would increase British reliance on the American nuclear guarantee. Britain would become increasingly dependent on America's nuclear weapons for its defence. But, the argument continues, it would be taking unfair advantage for Britain simply to shelter under the American 'nuclear umbrella' without attempting to share the costs and the risks attendant upon its own defence. Since the claim here is that, in giving up nuclear weapons, Britain would then be getting a 'free-ride' on the back of America's military strength, I shall call this argument the 'free-rider' argument.[21]

There is much that can be said in response to this argument — for example, that Britain might best contribute to its own defence, not by maintaining a meagre nuclear capacity, but by pursuing alternative, non-nuclear systems of defence. I shall return to this question later in Chapters III and IV.

For the moment, what is important to notice is that this argument is incompatible with each of the versions of the trigger argument. For, according to the trigger argument, TNW and independent weapons do not serve to relieve the US of part of the burden of the defence of Europe. On the contrary, any lightening of the American burden would be by definition 'decoupling' — precisely the phenomenon which these weapons are intended to guard against. For the role of Britain's nuclear weapons as defined by the trigger argument is simply to make certain that the US will come to the defence of Britain or Europe if their security is jeopardized. Thus, according to the trigger argument, Britain's nuclear weapons do not reduce Britain's dependence on the US; rather, they emphasize it.

Since the trigger and free-rider arguments are incompatible, they cannot both be used to support the retention of nuclear weapons. One of the arguments must be abandoned. I hope that what has been said thus far has been sufficient to cast serious doubt on the wisdom of using TNW or independent weapons as a catalyst for the engagement of American forces; so perhaps the trigger argument can be jettisoned. On the other hand, the free-rider argument will be persuasive only if nuclear weapons, in some role other than that of the trigger, are better suited to provide for British and European security needs than any other equally viable system of defence — otherwise the free-rider argument would itself support a non-nuclear option. Thus it remains to be seen whether proponents of nuclear weapons can turn the free-rider argument to their advantage. This will depend on the outcome of certain later arguments.

The Problem of Nuclear Blackmail

I mentioned earlier that there are two possible exceptions to Lord Carver's claim that it would never be reasonable for Britain to use nuclear weapons independently. The clearest of these two exceptions has already been discussed. This is the situation in which Britain has been so heavily bombed that it has little or nothing else to lose. I shall now discuss the second possible exception. The claim here is that it might be self-interestedly rational for Britain not only to threaten to use but actually to use nuclear weapons independently in the event that the Russians use nuclear blackmail against Britain. The argument which is based on this claim is obviously closely related to the second centre and last resort deterrent arguments. It is, however, so important an argument that it merits being treated separately.

It is rather difficult to draw a precise distinction between nuclear blackmail and nuclear deterrence.[22] I shall not go into the problems here, but shall simply adopt the provisional definition of nuclear blackmail as consisting in the threat to use nuclear weapons in order to coerce a country to act in a certain way desired by the blackmailer. The threat may be explicit or merely implicit.

It is sometimes argued that, if Britain were to relinquish independent nuclear weapons, the Soviet Union would then be free to use nuclear blackmail even in times of peace to gain British compliance with a wide range of demands. This would mean that much of Britain's freedom to act autonomously would have been lost. Perhaps this explains why proponents of nuclear weapons so often appeal to the ideal of liberty when arguing for their position. It seems to me, however, that there are strong political constraints which operate against the use of nuclear blackmail, and that these would be sufficient to prevent the Soviet Union from using it against Britain in times of peace. I shall not argue for this conclusion, but shall simply refer the reader to Robert Neild's excellent discussion of the problem in his book.[23]

The problem seems far more serious, however, when we consider that in times of war the immediate stakes might be so high that most of the political constraints against nuclear blackmail would simply vanish. It seems to me that the stakes in a European war would be so high that the threat of nuclear blackmail would be very real. There are primarily two ways in which nuclear blackmail might be used against Britain in the course of a European war. First, if a war were in progress in Central Europe in which British forces were engaged, the Russians could declare that, unless those British forces surrender, they (the Russians) will incinerate a major British city using nuclear weapons; then, if the forces still do not surrender, the Russians will incinerate another British city, and so on. If the British (as well as the Germans and others) could be compelled to surrender in this way, this would provide an easy victory for the Russians. Second, suppose that the Russians have succeeded in an invasion of Western Europe to the extent that they are at the Channel. They could then use the same threat in order to coerce the surrender of the forces deployed in the defence of British territory. In short, nuclear blackmail might be used to gain the surrender of British forces in Central Europe, thereby facilitating a Soviet military victory, or it might be used to gain the surrender of British forces deployed along the edges of British territory, thereby facilitating the domination and occupation of Britain by the Soviet Union.

The claim that is often made on behalf of Britain's independent strategic force is that it can serve to deter these forms of nuclear blackmail. For the Russians would never make the threat in the first place if they felt confident that Britain would retaliate to any strikes against British cities by striking Soviet cities. Again, however, whether or not the Russians will expect that retaliation would follow depends on how reasonable it would be for Britain to retaliate. So we must ask how reasonable it would be, if the Russians were to use nuclear blackmail, for Britain to refuse to capitulate, and to retaliate in the event that the Russians do destroy a British city.

If Britain would regard a high probability of losing a major city as an acceptable price to pay for the avoidance of an immediate defeat, then it might be reasonable for Britain not to surrender. (I say 'a high probability' because there is some chance that the Russians might be bluffing.) But once the Russians had destroyed a British city, it would then be necessary for Britain to retaliate; for, if Britain did not retaliate, the Russians would simply reiterate the threat and, unless Britain surrendered, would destroy another British city. In retaliating, Britain might hope that the Russians would be sufficiently impressed with Britain's resolve so as to be deterred from attempting nuclear blackmail a second time. So Britain would at least have a good reason for retaliating;

therefore the threat to retaliate has a certain amount of credibility in this situation.

An independent nuclear force therefore definitely has value as a deterrent against nuclear blackmail. To my mind, this constitutes a very strong reason for Britain to maintain an independent capacity — indeed, it seems to me to be overwhelmingly the strongest reason. Nevertheless, there are problems with this argument.

One problem with attempting to deter nuclear blackmail through the threat of retaliation is that the consequences could be appalling if deterrence fails. I have, of course, conceded that the consequences might be acceptable if deterrence fails in the first instance — that is, I have conceded that Britain might find it acceptable to sacrifice a city in order to avoid immediate defeat. The problem, however, is that, if deterrence fails once, it may fail again, perhaps eventually leading to the destruction of all of Britain. For, having gone this far, the Russians may not be persuaded to give up their attempt to force Britain to surrender. Remember that, in retaliating, Britain would probably have forfeited a submarine by revealing its location. So Britain would have at most two submarines left, and probably only one. If Britain has only one submarine left, then it would presumably not be reasonable for Britain to go on resisting. For suppose Britain resists and loses another city. Then to retaliate would be to reveal the location of its only remaining submarine. Thus to retaliate would be to risk being disarmed and then punitively annihilated.

This reasoning leads me to the following conclusion. A British independent nuclear force will serve as an entirely credible deterrent against nuclear blackmail only if Britain can be sure to have at least three boats at sea at the time that the blackmail threat might be made. For, if Britain has only one boat at sea, it could probably retaliate only once, after which it would be disarmed and therefore totally vulnerable to annihilation or occupation, whichever the Russians chose. So it would be irrational to retaliate. If, on the other hand, Britain has two boats at sea, it could retaliate twice. But, after retaliating once, it would probably lose one of its boats, and would then be in a position in which it would not be reasonable to retaliate. Anticipating this, Britain might not find it worthwhile to retaliate in the first instance. If, however, Britain has three boats at sea, the level of damage it could inflict on the Soviet Union on a 'tit-for-tat' basis before running out of weapons would be far too high for it to be worth it to the Russians to initiate the series of strikes and counterstrikes. Thus in this case the threat to retaliate in the first instance is highly credible.

The foregoing argument depends on the assumption that, if a submarine fires one of its missiles, the submarine runs a high risk of being located and destroyed. Given the advanced state of present ASW technology, this seems to be a plausible assumption. But it must be conceded that it is by no means *certain* that a submarine which fires a missile can be immediately located and destroyed. Thus if Britain has two submarines at sea, this will certainly be of *some* deterrent value against the threat of nuclear blackmail. My point is only that the deterrent value of two submarines may be relatively slight.

If it is right that Britain needs to keep three submarines at sea in order to maintain a fully credible deterrent against nuclear blackmail, then this obviously poses a problem. For, in order to be sure of being able to have three submarines at sea in a time of crisis, Britain would need to maintain a fleet of at least five and probably even six submarines. This would be enormously costly. In fact, even to be able to maintain a fleet of four submarines Britain will have to make significant reductions in the conventional forces which it commits to NATO operations. This fact itself presents a dilemma. If, in order to maintain even a minimal independent deterrent force, Britain must reduce its commitment to the conventional defence of Europe, then Britain will be purchasing an independent capacity at the expense of making it easier for the Russians to win a conventional war in Europe. And if the Russians can be fairly confident about winning a conventional war in Europe, then they will have less reason ever to use nuclear blackmail. In other words, in purchasing an independent deterrent against the threat of nuclear blackmail, Britain may be making it so that the Russians will never even need to use nuclear blackmail. On the other hand, if

Britain were to forgo the option of an independent deterrent and instead increase its conventional commitment to the defence of Europe, this would make it more difficult for the Russians to win a conventional war in Europe, and would therefore increase their incentive to use nuclear blackmail.

It seems to me that this dilemma can be avoided. If it is deemed necessary to have both strong conventional forces in Europe and the ability to deter nuclear blackmail in Europe, then it would seem that the way to meet these requirements is through a rational scheme of burden-sharing among the members of the Alliance. And it would seem to be a rational way of parcelling out the burdens to let Britain strengthen its conventional commitment to Europe's defence, while letting the Americans be responsible for the deterrence of nuclear blackmail in Europe. The reason for this is as follows. The US already has a vast retaliatory capability against the Soviet Union. It can maintain its ability to deter nuclear blackmail in Europe without damaging its own conventional capabilities in Europe or elsewhere. On the other hand, the US is experiencing problems maintaining sufficient manpower for its conventional forces both in Europe and elsewhere. It is also more difficult for the US than it is for Britain to transport troops and supplies to Central Europe. So it seems rather a waste of resources for Britain to try to duplicate America's capacity to deter nuclear blackmail at the cost of Britain's conventional forces — forces which the US would find it very difficult if not impossible to replace.

Now it may be objected to this proposal that an American threat to retaliate on Britain's behalf if nuclear blackmail is used against Britain will not be as credible as a British threat to retaliate would be. I concede that this is a problem, but I do not think that it is as serious as it seems at first sight. For one thing, we have already seen that a fleet of four submarines is itself not entirely credible as a deterrent against nuclear blackmail. There are, moreover, other factors which could seriously compromise the credibility of a British deterrent, but which are far less likely to damage the credibility of the American deterrent. Among these factors are possible advances in ASW or ABM technology. (The US has other deterrent forces besides submarines and ballistic missiles.)

There are, moreover, reasons for thinking that the American threat to retaliate would enjoy a reasonable measure of credibility. The main reason is that the US would be heavily committed to the conventional fighting in Europe, and would not be favourably disposed to the prospect of the British (and perhaps the German) armies being forced to surrender by the use of nuclear blackmail. In other words, it would be difficult for the Russians to blackmail Britain and Germany without also indirectly blackmailing the US. Indeed, if the British and American forces are fighting alongside each other, it may be difficult for the Russians to demand the surrender of the British troops without also demanding the surrender of the American troops. In this situation, the Russians would certainly have to think twice before engaging in nuclear blackmail against Britain. (This last argument admittedly applies only to the case in which the Russians use nuclear blackmail to gain the surrender of Britain's forces in Central Europe. I shall later suggest that there are other ways besides relying on nuclear weapons to attempt to deter the use of nuclear blackmail to gain the surrender of the British forces deployed in defence of British territory.)

A further thought which naturally arises here is that, if it would be more effective if Britain itself could threaten to retaliate, and the objection to this is only that Britain cannot afford to maintain a retaliatory capability, then why should not the US simply make Britain a present of, say, a fleet of five or six nuclear-armed submarines? There are two replies to this suggestion. First, the current US administration believes (to my mind quite wrongly) that it has a deficiency rather than a surplus of strategic weapons, and so it is unlikely to be in the right mood for giving part of its strategic arsenal away. Second, this proposal is politically unrealistic. It would be difficult for the US to give weapons to one of its allies without offering them to the others. It would, moreover, be very awkward for the US to give such dramatic recognition to Britain's need to defend itself against nuclear blackmail without also acknowledging a similar need on the part of West Germany. Yet no one would think it desirable for the US to provide West Germany with an independent nuclear capability.

Finally, it may be objected here that what I am recommending is that Britain should seek shelter underneath the American 'nuclear umbrella'. I accept this charge. When I later return to the problem of nuclear blackmail, I shall suggest why I think that Britain's reliance on the American guarantee would be very slight. For the moment, I shall simply suggest why the degree of reliance I have recommended here seems largely innocuous. The main point is that I am by no means recommending that Britain should be a free-rider. I am not advocating that Britain should not share the burdens of the defence of Europe, but only that the burdens should be allocated rationally between Britain and the US.

Normally when people object to Britain's being underneath the American nuclear umbrella they do so on moral grounds. They believe that it is immoral for Britain to rely for its defence on nuclear weapons, regardless of whether the nuclear weapons belong to Britain or to the US. I have considerable sympathy for this view, but when I later come to examine the various moral arguments against the possession of nuclear weapons, I shall explain why the two which would clearly condemn Britain's relying on the American nuclear guarantee are arguments which I cannot accept. There is one moral argument which I shall consider which I find more powerful, but it is not clear that this argument would condemn Britain's relying on the US to deter Soviet nuclear blackmail.

If what I have argued is correct, then even if nuclear weapons are needed in order to deter the possible use of nuclear blackmail in Europe, it does not follow that *Britain* should maintain a nuclear arsenal for this purpose. Nevertheless, the argument based on the threat of nuclear blackmail is a powerful one. I shall have more to say about it later in the book.

Arguments Concerning Prestige and Influence

Thus far all of the arguments we have considered, with the exception of the first version of the trigger argument, have been intended to support the possession by Britain of independent nuclear weapons. The three arguments to be considered in this section also purport to justify the retention of independent weapons, though the third argument is intended to support the retention of weapons in other categories as well. The arguments in this section are different from those considered earlier in that they focus on purely political rather than military considerations.

To call the first of these an 'argument' is actually a mistake. It does not deserve the dignity of that title. It is, nevertheless, too important to ignore altogether. It is the view that the possession of nuclear weapons serves to enhance Britain's stature as a world power. It is therefore feared that the renunciation of nuclear weapons would accelerate Britain's decline in the eyes of the world and — what is particularly galling — would leave France in the triumphant position of being the only European power to possess independent nuclear weapons.

Again, much could be said in response to this point. It is doubtful, for example, that nuclear weapons are everywhere regarded as a symbol of greatness. In some quarters they are regarded as a stigma. It is at least possible that, if Britain were to renounce nuclear weapons, this would not be viewed as a fall from glory, but would be welcomed as a bold initiative motivated by ideals which many of the world's inhabitants share. It might even help to dispel the all too prevalent view that Britain is merely a subservient client state of the US.

It is, however, difficult to take these anxieties about British prestige seriously. As a reason for having nuclear weapons (as opposed to an explanation of why we have them) the desire for prestige seems puerile and unworthy of serious attention. That is surely why this concern is rarely openly acknowledged by proponents of nuclear weapons. It is certainly not because considerations of prestige are without influence. The concern for prestige was undeniably one of the motives behind the initial British decision to acquire nuclear weapons. And who can honestly claim to believe that there are no politicians today whose opposition to disarmament is motivated, not so much by fear of the Russians, but by a desire to be seen as rulers of a Great Power?

If we agree that the desire for prestige is not a reason for having nuclear weapons, then there is no point in criticizing it further here. I have devoted space to discussing it only because, given that it does act as a stimulus to the arms race, it is clearly worthwhile to expose it to the contempt it deserves.

The next two arguments present us with a more interesting and serious set of considerations. These arguments are both versions of what I shall call the 'influence argument'. The first version can be seen as an extension of the previous argument concerning prestige. The idea is that there is a *reason* — other than merely to pander to national pride — why Britain should seek to maintain its current level of international prestige, and this is that Britain would otherwise have less influence over decisions taken in the US which bear on British and European interests.

What is again open to question, however, is the assumption that nuclear weapons provide the requisite sort of prestige — in this case, the sort which weighs heavily in American councils. The example of West Germany shows that the possession of nuclear weapons is not a necessary condition for exercising an important influence over American decision-making. And it is equally doubtful whether the possession of these weapons is itself sufficient to provide a high degree of influence: 'There are no known facts which indicate, let alone prove, that the Americans ever accepted a British suggestion because they [the British] had a Bomb.'[24]

The two versions of the influence argument can be seen as the positive and negative sides of the same argument: hence I shall refer to them as the 'positive' and 'negative' versions, respectively. The negative version holds, not that the possession of nuclear weapons is in itself responsible for Britain's influence over the formulation of American policy, but that nonetheless the renunciation of nuclear weapons would severely weaken the influence which Britain has until now been able to exercise.[25] The weakening of British influence would be a manifestation of the alienation which would arise between the two countries if Britain were to chart a more independent course in defence policy. The extent of this alienation would differ depending on which weapons systems

Britain were to give up. If only the independent weapons were abandoned, the impact on Anglo-American relations would probably be relatively slight. The Americans might even welcome the abandonment of the independent deterrent if this would mean that Britain could devote more of its resources to the conventional defence of Europe. But if, on the other hand, Britain were to refuse to employ NATO nuclear weapons, and in particular if it were to order the expulsion of American forward-based systems, then the hostility which would arise between the two countries could become serious. Thus, unlike the positive version, which argues almost exclusively for the retention of independent nuclear weapons, the negative version argues most strongly for the retention of American bases on British soil, and less strongly for the continued deployment of NATO TNW, and only rather weakly for retention of an independent nuclear capacity.

This negative version of the influence argument links up with the free-rider argument which we touched upon earlier. If Britain were to abandon some or all nuclear weapons without taking steps to compensate for their absence, it is easy to see how the Americans could regard this as an attempt by Britain to get a free-ride. This is one reason why the Americans would be hostile to British disarmament.

In assessing the force of this argument, we need to ask, first, how likely it is that Britain would lose its influence over the US if it were to give up nuclear weapons, and, second, how much it would matter even if Britain were to lose its influence. The examples of France and Canada both suggest that the weakening of Britain's influence would not be major. Both of these countries have expelled American forward-based systems from their soil, but neither has been banished from American councils as a result.

But even if Britain's influence would be significantly weakened, how much would this matter? There are two considerations which are relevant here: first, could the effects of Britain's influence, when assessed impartially, be expected to be benign? And, second, how much influence could Britain be expected to have even under favourable conditions? As to the first of these questions, my inclination is to think that the effects of Britain's influence would probably be on the whole beneficial — especially now that we are beginning to see the rebirth of a strident form of militarism in the US. It seems reasonable to assume that Britain could have a restraining or moderating influence on American policy.

I am less optimistic, however, about the impact which British counsels could be expected to have. On the whole, Britain's influence will be stronger the more agreement there is between the British and American governments on the major issues. We all tend to listen more attentively to those who for the most part share our own views, and the American Government is no exception to this. But this means that the greater Britain's capacity is to influence American behaviour, the fewer opportunities Britain will have to do so, since there will be fewer instances in which Britain and America will find themselves in disagreement. If, on the other hand, there were significant differences between the views of the British and American governments, there would then be ample opportunity for Britain to try to exercise an influence over the US, but little likelihood that Britain would in fact be listened to.

Suppose, for example, that a government sympathetic to British unilateral disarmament were to come to power in Britain during the years of the Reagan administration. Since it would believe that the Reagan administration was pursuing the wrong course, this government would obviously be keenly interested in trying to influence the direction of American defence and foreign policy. How strong a reason would it be for this government not to disarm if British disarmament might arouse intense American displeasure, and might therefore weaken the government's influence over the US? It seems to me that this alone would be only a rather weak reason for not disarming, since such a government would have only a very slight capacity for influencing American policy even if it were to retain nuclear weapons. It would not be the sort of government to which the Reagan administration would be inclined to listen in any case.

Now it might be thought that I am underestimating the

extent to which Britain can affect important decisions taken in the US. The classical example which is often brought forward to show just how influential Britain can be is the instance in which Attlee went to Washington to prevent Truman from using nuclear weapons during the Korean war. If Britain can prevent the US from acting rashly with regard to the use of nuclear weapons, then it is clearly important that Britain should not forfeit its access to Washington's ear.

I am inclined to doubt whether the example of Attlee actually establishes that much. It would appear from Truman's memoirs that Attlee's importance in this episode has been exaggerated. It is not at all clear that Truman ever intended to use nuclear weapons in Korea, or even that his implicit threat to do so was a calculated piece of nuclear blackmail.[26]

The Top Table Argument

A claim which is closely related to the positive version of the influence argument is that the independent possession of nuclear weapons provides 'a ticket of admission' to a 'seat at the top table'[27] in disarmament negotiations. This view appears in the 1960 White Paper, in which Macmillan's Defence Minister, Mr Watkinson, claimed that Britain's having nuclear weapons 'substantially increases our influence in negotiations for a nuclear test agreement, disarmament, and the reorganization of NATO strategy'.[28] Like the positive version of the influence argument, this 'top table argument' supports the retention only of independent weapons.

This view depends for its force on the assumption that the presence of British representatives has a salutary effect on the progress of disarmament negotiations. I am not myself sufficiently familiar with the history of arms control negotiations to know whether there are any instances in which Britain, in the context of negotiations, has forced the superpowers to make significant moves in the direction of disarmament which they probably would not otherwise have made. Given that very little was actually achieved in the area of arms control prior to the SALT negotiations, my inclination is to doubt that Britain can claim credit for any major achievements. Indeed, it is in general true that negotiations become more difficult and complicated the more negotiating parties there are. Since additional parties are usually an impediment, Britain might even be able to perform a more valuable service simply by giving up independent nuclear weapons unconditionally and withdrawing from further negotiations. In so doing Britain would certainly not be forfeiting the right to exert pressure on the superpowers to negotiate promptly and in good faith.

It should be mentioned here, as it almost invariably is whenever this argument is discussed, that the fact that Britain has been excluded from SALT shows that nuclear weapons do not always furnish a seat at the top table. On the other hand, however, it has been said that it is not so much that Britain was refused a seat at this particular top table, but that Britain actually did not want to participate in these negotiations. At least earlier in the SALT process the Soviet Union and probably even the United States would have welcomed British participation, but Britain was anxious to stay clear of the talks in order to exclude forward-based systems from the talks and in order to avoid having its independent forces bargained away.[29] So, it might be urged, the example of SALT does not falsify the claim that independent nuclear forces provide a seat at the top table.

Persons who attempt to defend the top table argument by claiming that Britain wished to avoid participating in SALT have failed to notice that this fact (if it is one) undermines their argument entirely: for why should Britain be so eager to have a ticket to the top table if it is unwilling to use it?

Perhaps aware that the case of SALT is rather an embarrassment for the top table argument, supporters of this argument have sometimes pointed to the Comprehensive Test Ban (CTB) negotiations as providing some justification for their view. David Owen, for example, has recently observed that 'in 1977 the Labour Government decided to be a full negotiating partner in the Comprehensive Test Ban negotiations with the US and USSR; that was the right way to use our nuclear position[:] not as a protester on the sidelines but as an active negotiator'.[30] This is a recent statement, but the actual outcome of these negotiations to date hardly warrants

Owen's enthusiasm. While the evidence does indeed suggest that Britain, or at least the last Labour Government, has been more anxious to reach an agreement than either of the two superpowers, the prospects for arriving at a significant treaty are now not favourable, and there is reason to believe that the Russians have exploited Britain's presence at the talks in engineering obstacles to the completion of the treaty. (They have, for example, insisted that Britain should meet certain preposterous conditions.[31])

It will be instructive, I think, to conclude this discussion of the top table argument by noting that the argument is nowadays being heard, not just in Britain, but in India as well. Recent reports confirm that India has been preparing for a second nuclear explosive test, so that there can now be no doubt that India intends to develop its own nuclear arsenal as soon as possible. Indeed, the Indians seem no longer concerned to deny this. Propaganda in favour of the Indian bomb has therefore begun to pour forth from India, and one of the points which has recently been made (by the Director of the Defence Studies Institute in India) is that 'possession of its own nuclear arsenal would not only raise India's international prestige, but would force other countries to listen seriously when it argued for disarmament'.[32]

India is here championing what Robin Cook has called 'the multilateralist paradox — that we must first build a bomb of our own in order to play a constructive part in banning it'.[33] But, if this claim on behalf of India strikes us as a mere rationalization, a cynical and unashamed piece of hypocrisy, then imagine how all this prating about the 'top table' by British politicians has all along sounded to people in non-nuclear countries. If India's present action argues much more strongly against disarmament than anything that India might say in favour of disarmament, the same is true of Britain's past and present action.

It is revealing that in this piece of Indian propaganda the concern for prestige appears side by side with the top table argument. It is difficult to avoid the suspicion that the importance which politicians attach to having a seat at the top table (and it is from politicians that we most often hear this argument) stems not so much from a desire to get rid of nuclear weapons, but from a mere desire to be accorded the privileges befitting the representatives of a Great Power. These politicians claim that their real aim is to get rid of nuclear weapons, but one is tempted to reply that, if this is what they want to do, why then do they not, with respect to their own weapons at least, just do it?

The Multilateralist's Argument

There is in fact a good answer to the question I have just posed. One reason for thinking that Britain ought not simply to bypass negotiations and disarm unilaterally is that, if British nuclear weapons could instead be given up in the context of a negotiated, multilateral disarmament process, their renunciation could then be traded for similar concessions on the part of the Soviet Union. Clearly, this would be a greater step in the direction of overall disarmament. It is for this reason that David Owen has claimed that proponents of unilateral disarmament 'underestimate ... the extent to which large unilateral steps towards disarmament will actually impede progress in overall disarmament. Large steps ... remove the incentive from some countries to negotiate matching responses . . . .'[34]

This 'multilateralist's argument' is undoubtedly important. While it militates against the unilateral abandonment of nuclear weapons in any category, it is perhaps strongest in the case of the proposed 160 cruise missiles. It has often been suggested (though not by the Defence Ministry) that one of the reasons for having cruise missiles is that they will provide a 'bargaining chip' which can be traded against the Soviet SS20 intermediate-range ballistic missiles (IRBMs) targeted on Western Europe. It is held, in other words, that at present the West has nothing to trade in return for reductions in the number of SS20s; therefore we should install cruise missiles in order to abolish them along with the SS20s. Since the cruise missiles will be controlled solely by the US, they will be more worrying to the Russians than Britain's *Polaris* or *Trident* force. The offer to withdraw them is therefore more likely to secure significant Soviet concessions than the offer to withdraw the independent force.

The multilateralist's argument has the appearance of good sense, but it ignores two vital considerations: first, that negotiations have in the past achieved very little, and second, that negotiations take a long time, and time is fast running out. Simple induction bids us not to put all our faith in a process which in the past has proven repeatedly to have been a barren and time-consuming exercise in futility. Robin Cook's judgement on the history of arms control is sadly accurate: 'Such negotiations have been going on more or less incessantly ... and have miserably failed either to disarm a single warhead or even to prevent a fearsome growth in the arsenals of the superpowers.'[35]

Consider, for example, the Mutual and Balanced Force Reductions talks (MBFR), which are talks aimed at reducing force levels in Central Europe. These talks began officially in 1973, though the negotiators had been conducting preparatory talks for four years prior to this time. Even after twelve years of talks the negotiators have still been unable to agree even on certain preliminary matters of definition. This is not an aberration. It is a typical feature of arms control negotiations that it takes years and years for the participants to be able to agree on such basic matters as what weapons belong in which categories, what counts as 'equivalence' within a category, and so on.

It is common for politicians to insist that we must simply be patient, that we must allow them time in which to pursue the painstaking process of negotiation. There is, however, a certain amount of audacity in asking us to believe that, after twenty years of relative failure, they will this time achieve something of real significance. We waited patiently for seven years for SALT II, only to have the completed treaty rejected by the Reagan administration.

There are even reasons for doubting whether these politicians are actually sincere in their claim to want to see multilateral disarmament achieved. If it is true that the British Government was anxious to avoid becoming involved in SALT for fear that Britain's weapons would be traded away for Soviet concessions, then we are certainly entitled to be sceptical when politicians today assure us that they are eager to disarm if only the Russians would cooperate.

If we grant that proponents of the second centre argument, the last resort deterrent argument, and so on, are sincere in their espousal of these arguments, then it is difficult to avoid doubting their sincerity if they simultaneously espouse the multilateralist's argument. For, if they believe that there are strong military and strategic reasons for having an independent deterrent, then it is doubtful whether any feasible arms control agreement could offer a sufficient inducement for relinquishing this deterrent. The concessions which could be gained from the Soviet Union in exchange for giving up the independent deterrent would not be sufficient to eliminate the reasons these people think there are for having the deterrent. Even after the most advantageous bargain possible had been struck, the Soviet arsenal would remain relatively untouched. There would still be a Soviet threat. There would still be a possibility of nuclear blackmail. If defenders of British nuclear weapons honestly believe, as they say they do, that these weapons have in the past helped to preserve peace, how then can they claim to want to abolish them?

There is, in other words, a sense in which the multilateralist's argument is incompatible with the strategic arguments we considered earlier. This is perhaps true only in the case of the smaller nuclear powers like Britain and France. The superpowers have a vast superfluity of nuclear weapons (often referred to as an 'overkill' capacity), and could happily reduce their stockpiles in an equal and balanced way without compromising their security. But Britain has only a relatively small number of nuclear weapons. If one takes the military and strategic arguments for having these weapons seriously, then one cannot regard any of these weapons as surplus which can be traded away in a scheme of mutual reductions. One would have to regard any genuinely balanced reduction as being to Britain's disadvantage.

Suppose for the moment, however, that the British Government is sincere in wanting negotiations, and would be willing to phase out Britain's nuclear weapons in return for matching Soviet reductions. What are the prospects at present for achieving significant results in the area of arms control and negotiated disarmament? It is important to bear in mind here that Britain does not act autonomously in this sphere. Britain does not conduct negotiations with the Soviet Union on its own, but must instead be accompanied by (some might say supervised by) the US. So even the best of intentions on Britain's part would not be sufficient even to set negotiations into motion. Britain, it seems, must await America's pleasure.

But the US is at the moment poised on the brink of the most massive programme of peacetime rearmament in American history. The Reagan administration's defence budget calls for a 50 per cent increase in defence spending by 1986. This will involve the allocation of over one and a half million million dollars to defence over the next five years. The administration's aim, according to Mr Weinberger, is to restore American military superiority over the Soviet Union. Clearly, the US is in no mood to negotiate reductions with the Soviet Union. Indeed, Mr Weinberger seems to have rejected arms control altogether. At a NATO meeting in April of 1981, Weinberger claimed that Russia had taken advantage of the period of détente in order to accumulate arms on a larger scale than during the previous era of the Cold War. He is reported to have said that, 'if movement from Cold War to détente was progress, then let me say that we can't afford more progress'.[36] A few weeks before this, a member of Reagan's National Security Council announced that 'détente is dead', and claimed that the Reagan administration believes that negotiations with the Russians are pointless unless the Russians begin to behave in a way more acceptable to the US.[37] Finally, Reagan himself recently stated that

No nation that placed its faith in parchment or paper while at the same time it gave up its protective hardware ever lasted long enough to write many pages in history . . . The argument, if there is any, will be over which weapons, and not whether we should forsake weaponry for treaties and agreements.[38]

It is true, of course, that in early May of 1981 Alexander Haig, the American Secretary of State, pledged at a NATO meeting in Rome to set a date for reopening talks with the Soviet Union on nuclear weapons in Europe. No one doubts, however, that this was merely a cosmetic gesture designed to weaken public opposition in Europe to the 1979 NATO decision to station cruise missiles and *Pershing II*s in Europe. This pledge was strongly opposed in Washington, and it is clear that it would never have been obtained if West European governments had not made it clear to the US that public pressure might prevent them from being able to implement the 1979 decision unless the US showed a willingness to negotiate.

Given the prevailing attitudes in the US, it is highly unlikely that, even with the best of intentions, Britain will be able to achieve anything of significance in the areas of arms control and disarmament. In terms of reducing present stockpiles of nuclear weapons, there is certainly no prospect of achieving through negotiation anything as significant as British unilateral nuclear disarmament would be.

With something like the multilateralist's argument in mind, Aneurin Bevan once vowed that he would not go naked into the conference chamber. This memorable phrase has often been repeated. Only recently has an editorial writer for *The Guardian* produced what seems an appropriate rejoinder: 'We are fully clothed but where is the conference?'[39]

Thus far I have argued that the future promises very few opportunities for arriving at multilateral agreements. But, for the sake of argument, let us make the optimistic assumption that there will be ample opportunities for negotiation. I shall argue that, even if we grant this assumption, the exclusive pursuit of multilateral solutions may serve only to fuel the arms race.

Because multilateral negotiations require time, the pursuit of these negotiations will require vigorous 'modernization' programmes — which means that Britain's nuclear arsenal will be expanding all the time that negotiations are taking place. There are two reasons for this. The first is that Britain will need to maintain the credibility of its deterrent throughout the protracted period of negotiation, and many of Britain's present systems (for example, the *Vulcans*) are rapidly declining into obsolescence. The second reason is that the

West will feel compelled to pursue the development and deployment of new weapons in order to be able to 'bargain from a position of strength'.

As we have seen, it has been said that the desire to bargain from a position of strength has at least partly motivated the decision to deploy cruise missiles in England. This same desire has probably also influenced the decision to replace *Polaris* with *Trident*. Unless Britain now sets in motion the process whereby *Polaris* will be replaced by *Trident*, then by the early 1990s, when the oldest *Polaris* submarines will cease to be operable, Britain will be without an independent deterrent. So unless Britain presses ahead with the *Trident* programme now, the Russians will lack an incentive to bargain for the abandonment of Britain's independent capacity. There is no reason to offer concessions for the abandonment of a system which will soon be obsolete.

There is reason to fear, however, that both the cruise missiles and *Trident* will share the fate of previous 'bargaining chips'. In order to serve as a bargaining chip, a weapons system must be in the process of being developed and deployed. Merely to threaten the development of the system is generally insufficient. But 'once a weapon is under development, it acquires a constituency of military, political, and industrial advocates who resist efforts at stopping its deployment no matter what the results of negotiations with the other great power may be'.[40] It was this consideration which led the participants at the 1972 Pugwash conference in Oxford to declare, with reference to SALT, that,

If future negotiations should be used as an excuse or argument for new or expanded strategic arms programs, so as to be able to negotiate from a position of strength, we question whether such negotiations would be worthwhile. An effort to accumulate such 'bargaining chips' for use during negotiations could result in a growth in strategic weapons so great as to offset any advantages that might result from eventual agreements.[41]

A similar scepticism may well be warranted in the present case. It is hard to believe that, once the necessary time, effort, and money have been invested in the production of cruise missiles and *Trident*, our leaders will be willing to turn around and discard these weapons as soon as the Russians offer to make a matching concession.

I have given a long and rather complicated reply to the multilateralist's argument, so I shall now try to summarize the main points I have made. First, I claimed that there is reason for doubting whether politicians are actually being candid with us when they claim to support British disarmament in the context of a multilateral agreement. Their beliefs about the political and military importance of having nuclear weapons seem to pull them strongly in the other direction. Second, I argued that, even if we could be sure that our leaders sincerely desired negotiated disarmament, the attitude of the US towards disarmament negotiations is at present such that the prospects for opening serious negotiations with the Russians are very unpromising. Third, I claimed that, even if the prospects for negotiations were favourable, the negotiations themselves would take many years and might in the end fail to produce significant results. All the while the arms race would be accelerating, so that the net result of the negotiations might be a situation worse than that with which we began.

The moral of my argument is not that arms control should be abandoned. On the contrary, it should be vigorously pursued, especially by the superpowers: otherwise it is very difficult to see how greater stability can be reestablished in superpower relations. My point is only that, in addition to arms control, bold initiatives are required if we are to escape from our present predicament. These will have to be unilateral initiatives. I have tried to show that the multilateralist's claim that more can be achieved if we forgo acting unilaterally is, in the present circumstances, not borne out by the evidence.

Finally, it should be mentioned that there is some ground for hoping that British unilateral moves might themselves provide the Russians with an incentive for making matching, or at least similar responses. For, if Britain's gesture were to be perceived by the Russians as an act of good will, intended at least in part to ease tensions and to facilitate further action of the same sort, then they might feel compelled to reciprocate — for propaganda purposes if for no more meritorious reasons.[42]

The Problem of Germany

It is often said that Britain's European allies regard the British independent deterrent as a 'back-up' defence which provides some measure of insurance against the failure of the American nuclear guarantee. In other words, the allies regard the independent force, not so much as a last resort *national* deterrent, but as a last resort *European* deterrent. While this view has often been criticized on the ground that Britain would never initiate a nuclear exchange with Russia in defence of, say, West Germany, this criticism misses the important point that Britain's security is inextricably bound up with the security of Western Europe as a whole. So, if the British are entitled to feel that the independent force strengthens *their* security, the European allies should be entitled to feel that at least some protection extends to them as well.

Now, in itself the assumption that Britain's European allies value Britain's having an independent deterrent is not an argument. But it provides the basis for what seems to me a powerful argument in favour of Britain's continuing to maintain an independent nuclear capability. The argument is that the reassurance which the British weapons provide helps to reduce the temptation on the part of the European allies to acquire nuclear weapons of their own. Thus if Britain were to disarm — in particular if Britain were to give up its independent capability — this might provide a sufficient incentive to other European countries to build their own bombs. Many of these countries have the economic and technological resources to develop an independent nuclear arsenal at relatively short notice. The West Germans, in particular, could 'go nuclear' more quickly and easily than perhaps any country on earth. And if the West Germans were to succumb to the pressure to develop a nuclear arsenal, the resulting situation would be far worse than the *status quo*.

The Russians have repeatedly stated, in terms which make it impossible to doubt their sincerity, that they would find it intolerable for West Germany to become a nuclear power. In part this stems from a general and deeply ingrained mistrust of the Germans which a familiarity with recent history makes readily understandable. More specifically, there is the fear that the nuclear-arming of West Germany could foster a mood of national assertiveness, and perhaps even lead to a revival of Nazism, which could then unfold into a campaign to reunite the two Germanies by force, and so on. (These fears would be heightened if, as would probably be the case, the drive to acquire nuclear weapons were to come at a time of domestic unrest occasioned by economic decline.) In any event, it is not improbable that, if the Germans were to initiate a nuclear arms programme, the Russians would, if not launch an invasion, at least conduct preemptive strikes against West German munitions facilities and weapons installations.

If the assumptions of this argument are correct, then to my mind the argument provides a strong reason for Britain to maintain an independent nuclear capacity.[43] I would accept the view that, if it were clear that British disarmament would spur the West Germans to build their own nuclear arsenal, then Britain ought not to disarm — since this would increase rather than decrease the likelihood of nuclear war. At a minimum, this argument shows that, if Britain is to disarm, it must be in close consultation with the West Germans.

It is possible, however, to challenge the fundamental assumption of this argument — namely, that the European allies and West Germany in particular feel that the British independent deterrent greatly enhances their own security. In the speech before the House of Lords which I quoted earlier, Lord Carver stated that

but do they?

It is often said that our allies welcome the fact that we have such a force. I have never heard an author[it]ative military or political figure of any of our allies welcome the fact officially that we have an independent strategic force.[44]

One can even find statements expressing scepticism about the military value for Western Europe of the British force. For example, two Dutch parliamentarians have stated that 'the UK's nuclear forces as currently structured would contribute little to the credibility of a European defence'.[45] I have myself come across only one statement from a West German source expressing enthusiasm over Britain's independent force:

> The possession by the United Kingdom of strategic nuclear weapons is considered to be an advantage by most, if not all, non-nuclear weapons countries of NATO, as it provides for a 'European voice' in the nuclear affairs of the Alliance and prevents a (politically unwelcome) state of US-monopoly. This British contribution is therefore of primary importance.[46]

It is important that the emphasis in this quotation is on the *political* importance of the British force. Lord Carver, in the same speech, concedes that

> I have indeed heard [our allies] welcome the fact that we are in the nuclear business, because, whether they are Americans or European[s], they believe that the fact that America is not alone in this is of great political value. But it is not necessarily o[f] military value.

This is important because it is unlikely that, if Britain were to disarm, any of the allies would be tempted to acquire nuclear weapons for purely political reasons — for example, to prevent there being an American monopoly within the Alliance. The West Germans, in particular, could hardly be tempted by political considerations, for the political value of a West German bomb would on balance be distinctly negative.

It would seem, therefore, that the foregoing argument overestimates the impact which British disarmament would have in West Germany. Let us suppose, however, that British disarmament would in fact be very alarming to the Germans. Could anything be said to them which might assuage their fears and discourage them from pursuing a potentially suicidal course? By rehearsing the reasons why the threat of British independent use lacks credibility in most situations, one might persuade the Germans that they would stand to lose little if Britain were to abandon its independent deterrent. This might, however, be self-defeating, in that it might itself convince the Germans of the necessity of looking after themselves. On the other hand, they might reason that, if Britain does not find its independent deterrent worth having, then they might not find their own deterrent worth having.

The most sensible course would be to attempt to demonstrate to the Germans the cogency of the reasoning which had led Britain to want to disarm. Of course, this would not work if Britain's reasons were essentially self-interested. But, if Britain had become convinced that both British and European security would be enhanced if Britain were, for example, to devote all of its resources to conventional defences, then it might be possible to persuade the Germans that they would be better off if Britain were to 'go conventional'. Whether the British would in fact be warranted in arguing this way is a subject to which I shall return in later sections of this book.

The Contribution to NATO Argument

It is often noted that Britain's nuclear weapons — in particular the independent deterrent — constitute 'a contribution to NATO's nuclear deterrent'. (Providing bases for American weapons is also part of Britain's contribution.) Within this description lies an argument which closely resembles the earlier free-rider argument and which may be set out schematically as follows:

(a) It is in Britain's interests to belong to the NATO alliance.
(b) But for Britain to derive the benefits of membership in the Alliance while failing to do its share to maintain the strength of the Alliance's defences would be unfair to the other members.
(c) In order to contribute most effectively to the strength

of the Alliance's defences, Britain ought to retain possession of certain nuclear weapons. Therefore:

(d) Britain ought to have nuclear weapons.

This argument is subtly different from the free-rider argument. The free-rider argument holds that Britain ought to share certain of the costs and risks of the defence of Europe even if not doing so would not damage the effectiveness of the Alliance's defences (because the other members would make up for the loss of Britain's contribution). But the contribution to NATO argument holds that Britain ought to share the burdens of the common defence, not just because not to do so would place a greater burden on the other members, but also because not to do so would impair the effectiveness of the Alliance's defences.

I shall not dispute the first two premisses of this argument. And, since the third premiss will be examined in considerable detail later in the book, we must await the outcome of that later discussion before we can judge how compelling the 'contribution to NATO argument' actually is. For the moment it may be illuminating to examine the ways in which this argument is related to certain of the other arguments I have already considered.

In the 1963 Defence White Paper there is a reference to Britain's 'independent contribution'.[47] This oxymoron reveals a certain schizophrenia in official thinking about the role of Britain's independent nuclear weapons which certain commentators have not failed to notice. One writer has even claimed that 'a full commitment to NATO is logically incompatible with an independent capability in any form'.[48] This seems too strong. There is a certain amount of tension in the claim that Britain contributes to NATO by maintaining weapons that are to some extent independent of NATO control; but the claim is not contradictory. Recall the second centre argument. If that argument were persuasive, then the Alliance as a whole would benefit more from Britain's retaining independent control over certain weapons than it would if Britain were to place these weapons totally under NATO control. Indeed, I am inclined to think that it is only as *independent* weapons that Britain's strategic forces could make a significant contribution to the security of the Alliance. When considered, not as an independent force, but simply as a component of NATO's strategic force, the British SLBMs fade into insignificance alongside the American component. As Robin Cook has noted, 'were the Polaris force eliminated its effect on NATO's strategic forces would barely be noticed'.[49] If the Russians will be undeterred by the American forces, they will not be deterred by the presence of one or two additional submarines.

Where the contribution to NATO argument runs into most trouble is in its relation to the trigger argument.[50] Earlier I argued that the trigger argument is incompatible with the free-rider argument. So, if the contribution to NATO argument is similar to the free-rider argument, then it should not be surprising if it is not altogether compatible with the trigger argument.[51] The trigger argument holds that the British independent forces are an instrument for involving the US in a war which it wishes to avoid. But this function could hardly be regarded as a 'contribution' to NATO. The notion that British forces are a contribution to NATO implies that they are harmoniously and cooperatively integrated into the structure of NATO forces. But to force a member state of NATO into a war against its will is not a cooperative act.

If we reject the trigger argument, as I earlier suggested we should do, then this will solve the problem of incompatibility. But it will be open to us to embrace the contribution to NATO argument only if its third premiss is sound. I shall turn to this question in the next chapter.

III

ARGUMENTS FOR THE
ABANDONMENT OF
NUCLEAR WEAPONS

In the last chapter I examined in detail a number of arguments in favour of Britain's having nuclear weapons. It might be thought, however, that I failed to meet head-on the wider question of whether the renunciation of nuclear weapons by Britain would, all things considered, have the effect of reducing British and European security. My criticisms of the foregoing arguments have, I think, shown that the case for having nuclear weapons is much weaker than many people suppose. But, as we have seen, each of the military arguments has a certain amount of force, so that together they may add up to a fairly plausible case. It would clearly be difficult to deny that the nuclear weapons in Britain have a certain amount of value as a deterrent. Someone might therefore say that, while nuclear weapons are admittedly of limited value in meeting the Soviet threat, simply to eliminate them would only leave us more exposed than before; so, unless there is a better alternative, we should simply make the best of a bad situation.

The first argument for the abandonment of nuclear weapons confronts this challenge head-on.

Alternatives to Reliance on Nuclear Weapons

The claim of this first argument is that there *are* better ways of defending Britain and Europe against the Soviet threat than using or threatening to use nuclear weapons. It should be emphasized at the outset, however, that this argument is confined to the consideration of alternative defence policies for Britain only. It is, perhaps, implicit in this argument that it would also be better for other West European countries to adopt non-nuclear policies. But the explicit claim of the argument is only that it would strengthen British and European security if Britain were to adopt a non-nuclear defence policy, regardless of whether or not other European countries were to continue to deploy nuclear weapons.

Although I have spoken of *an* alternative defence policy for Britain, I shall not in fact advance a single, particular proposal. I shall instead mention certain possible non-nuclear modes of defence, and suggest that they have certain advantages over nuclear weapons. If the balance of advantages seems to favour a non-nuclear policy, then the best policy for Britain will presumably be composed of a mixture of elements drawn from the various modes of defence I shall consider. I am not competent to judge which particular blend of elements would be best. However, the recently formed Alternative Defence Commission based at Bradford University will be publishing a report of its findings in the Spring of 1982, and I understand that they expect to recommend a particular mixture of various types of non-nuclear defence. This will be far more authoritative and well-grounded than anything I could offer here. The argument of this section should therefore be regarded as a modest and tentative effort in an area in which better-researched and more thorough work is to be published soon.

In order to determine whether a non-nuclear defence policy would be superior to a policy involving reliance on nuclear weapons, it is necessary to know what are the relevant standards for comparison. Leaving aside economic and purely political considerations, there are, I suggest, at least four criteria which are of paramount importance in comparing the merits of the two types of policy. These are:

(1) Under which of the two policies would the risk of nuclear war in Europe be less?

(2) Under which policy would the risk of conventional war in Europe be less?

(3) Under which policy would the risk of Britain's being dominated or occupied by a foreign power be less?

(4) Under which policy would the expected damage resulting from a war in Europe be less?

I shall not attempt to compare a non-nuclear defence policy with a policy involving reliance on nuclear weapons until the end of the book. This is mainly because such a comparison cannot be fairly conducted until we have considered all the various arguments against nuclear weapons. Therefore this first argument against nuclear weapons will have to be regarded as open-ended or inconclusive until I eventually come to conduct the relevant comparison. But it is nevertheless worthwhile to make these criteria explicit at the outset in order to provide a focus or point of reference for any judgements we may be in a position to make before then.

The goal which receives most emphasis in these criteria is, of course, the prevention of war. The primary purpose of a defence policy is to prevent war by deterring it. (There are, of course, other ways of preventing war than by deterring it, but these other ways fall within the province of diplomacy rather than defence.) There are, furthermore, two ways of deterring war. One is through what one writer calls 'the threat of gain denial' and the other is through 'the threat of resource destruction'. The notions of 'gain denial' and 'resource destruction' are explained in the following way:

> 'Gain denial' is the ability to deny the adversary his military objectives — specifically in regard to NATO, the seizure of territory and the control of population and resources. This mode of deterrence involves the ability to destroy tactical and other military targets, including forces in the field. 'Resource destruction' refers to the ability (in retaliation for aggression) to destroy resources highly valued by the adversary leadership but which do not immediately affect Warsaw Pact capability to seize NATO territory ... Gain-denial threats deter by reducing the adversary's perceived gain from aggression; resource-destruction threats deter by increasing his perceived loss.[1]

Following Dan Smith, I shall refer to these two modes of deterrence as 'defensive deterrence' and 'retaliatory deterrence', respectively.[2]

The types of alternative defence I shall sketch are entirely defensive; they make no provision for retaliation. So any measure of retaliatory deterrence currently provided by Britain's nuclear weapons would be lost if Britain were to adopt a non-nuclear defence policy along these lines. But, while Britain would lose the ability to deter aggression through the threat of retaliation, it would not lose its ability to *defend* itself. Indeed, Britain's ability to defend itself would be increased by the types of alternative defence I shall now explore. The idea is that, by strengthening defensive deterrence, Britain might be able to make up for the loss of retaliatory deterrence.[3]

Stronger Conventional Defences

The most obvious step which Britain could take in order to fill the gap left by the renunciation of nuclear weapons would be to strengthen its conventional forces. The details of how this would be best carried out are complicated and controversial, so I shall mention only a few general points which are relevant to my main line of argument.

In part Britain's conventional forces could be strengthened simply by reassigning present nuclear weapons delivery systems to conventional roles. With the exception of *Polaris* and *Lance*, all of these systems are already capable of delivering conventional explosives. And even the *Lance* missiles might be fitted with conventional warheads. But certain new and different types of weapon would also be required.

Conventional planning should be geared primarily towards repelling a conventional Warsaw Pact invasion. (The fact that Warsaw Pact forces will be equipped with nuclear weapons must of course be taken into account. I shall return to this shortly.) In the event of such an invasion, NATO forces would enjoy certain natural advantages. Vice-Admiral Sir Peter Gretton has recently stated that

When studying and teaching at various defence academies, I learnt that a successful land offensive must have a superiority of at least four to one. The advantages are all with the defence.[4]

These natural advantages can be augmented by the deployment of what are known as 'precision-guided munitions' (PGM). These are conventionally-armed battlefield weapons which, because of recent revolutions in guidance technology, have achieved an extremely high degree of accuracy.[5] PGM are often referred to as 'smart bombs', since they are capable of homing in on their targets. Dan Smith has written that

> the large-scale deployment of PGM in ground forces must be concluded to be more advantageous to the defence than to the offence, asymmetrically favouring infantry and other anti-tank units more than armoured forces. There is at present no alternative to the tank to form the core of major offensives; were a W[arsaw] P[act] offensive ever to occur, tanks can be expected to be the major component of combined arms teams. Weaponry which helps to neutralise the effectiveness of tanks therefore provides crucial capabilities to defensive forces in their major task . . .[6]

It would seem, therefore, that Britain ought to contribute to the upgrading of NATO's armoury of precision-guided anti-tank and anti-aircraft missiles.

Britain's conventional defences might be strengthened in either or both of two areas. On the one hand, greater efforts might be focused on the defence of British territory; on the other, more conventional forces might be committed to the Central Region of Europe. Both the problem of Germany and the contribution to NATO argument (see the last two sections of Chapter II) suggest that a strong British commitment to the defence of Central Europe is vital. And, after all, it is in Central Europe that an invasion would begin, and it makes sense to attempt to have sufficient forces at the borders of NATO territory to contain and repel an invasion at that point.

An increase in Britain's contribution to NATO's conventional forces in Central Europe might be regarded by Britain's

European allies as a more welcome contribution to the defence of Europe than, say, *Trident*. (If so, this would of course solve the problem of Germany.) One reason the allies might have for preferring an increased conventional commitment is that having stronger conventional forces would enable Western leaders, in the event of a European war, to prolong the period before they would feel pressured to escalate to the nuclear level. This in turn means that they would have more time to try by diplomatic means to bring the war to a close before it reached catastrophic proportions.

The suggestion that Britain should strengthen its conventional defences is, of course, not without problems. Perhaps the main problem is that it might be very expensive. I shall return to this in a later section of the chapter. Another problem is that it might prove 'decoupling': for, the more capable Europe is of taking care of itself, the less America will feel compelled to risk destruction by coming to Europe's defence. It seems to me, however, that an increased British conventional capability would not be significant enough in military terms to be decoupling. This problem would threaten to arise only if other West European states were to follow Britain's example. Finally, there is the very important problem that having a strong conventional defence could lead the Russians to use nuclear weapons in an effort to overcome it.[7] It is the awareness of this problem which leads us to consider a second form of defence.

Protection for Military Assets

In order for strengthened conventional forces to serve as a credible defensive deterrent, precautions must be taken to insure that there is a maximal probability that these forces will be able to survive an attack by a nuclear-armed aggressor. There are three basic types of precaution which may be taken: dispersal, concealment, and hardening of one's military assets.

The first two of these measures are based on the simple assumption that the Warsaw Pact will not use nuclear weapons for military purposes unless NATO provides them with suitable nuclear targets. Thus, one West German writer has argued that,

If an enemy has weapons which can cause unacceptable damage, and which cannot be intercepted, then rational strategy requires care to be taken that the enemy does not find a meaningful ... military use for these weapons ... An option for defence is [therefore] rational from the standpoint of the West European countries only if it sets up no military interest for the W[arsaw] T[reaty] O[rganization] to make use of nuclear weapons should deterrence fail ... [T]he WTO has ... an extremely great interest in the use of nuclear weapons if it can smash NATO's defences with nuclear weapons, and only with nuclear weapons. Therefore defence strategies which can be knocked out by nuclear weapons and only by nuclear weapons should not be established.[8]

British conventional forces not stationed along the front lines should therefore be dispersed to the maximum possible extent over wide areas rather than concentrated in particular, conspicuous locations. Small (and mobile) concentrations of weapons and troops scattered throughout the country would not present the Warsaw Pact with targets worth attacking with nuclear weapons. An attempt should also be made to conceal the locations of these smaller concentrations, though for obvious reasons this is for the most part impossible during times of peace.

Clearly, dispersal and concealment are not possible for all types of military asset. In cases in which these measures are not possible, and military assets must be concentrated in fixed locations, efforts should be made to 'harden' both weapons and vital facilities against the effects of a nuclear attack. Hardening programmes are in fact being implemented at present at various US air bases in Britain. For example, reinforced underground hangars are being built for certain planes. It is also important to try to acquire weapons systems which do not rely on facilities which are highly vulnerable to nuclear destruction. Thus vertical take-off planes or 'jump-jets' would be valuable acquisitions, since they do not require long runways in order to take off.

Although it would certainly be worthwhile to take pre-cautions of these sorts, the Warsaw Pact would have obvious reasons for wanting to keep the use of nuclear weapons at a minimum. As one American strategist has put it, the Warsaw Pact 'would have incentive to avoid unnecessary destruction of nonmilitary areas in order not to impede the rapid advance of their armored forces and in order to preserve economic resources for the postwar use of the conquerors'.[9]

Civil Defence

It is not just the military, but also the civilian population that should be protected as much as possible from the effects of both conventional and nuclear attacks. Thus the defence arrangements which might serve to supplant reliance on nuclear weapons should, I believe, include large-scale civil defence programmes.

This advocacy of civil defence may raise a few hackles among persons involved in the present disarmament campaign. But opposition to civil defence in the circumstances I am envisaging would, I think, be a mistake. There is a tremendous difference between civil defence for a nuclear-armed state and civil defence for a non-nuclear state. I shall cite several reasons for thinking that civil defence is undesirable for a nuclear-armed state. It will then be clear why these reasons are inapplicable in the case of non-nuclear states. This will help to explain why persons in the disarmament movement are opposed to the current civil defence planning for Britain. This is something which needs to be explained, for civil defence appears to many people to be simply a humane and purely defensive measure, and it is therefore puzzling to them when civil defence preparations are opposed.

One very important reason why civil defence preparations are undesirable in a nuclear-armed state is that they may be misunderstood by a potential enemy as a preparation for war. If a country intended to launch a first strike, one thing it would do would be to engage in civil defence preparations in order to enable it to survive any retaliation that might come. This is why civil defence preparations in the US or the Soviet Union appear so ominous and alarming to the other side. Of course, the Russians would not interpret British civil defence as an indication that Britain was preparing to launch an offensive war all by itself. But it might be seen as a sign that preparations for war were being made within the NATO alliance, or by Britain's close ally, the US. And one reason why it is best to avoid alarming the Soviet leaders and exacerbating their suspicions is that, the more nervous and mistrustful they are, the more likely it is that they will panic and act irrationally in a time of crisis.

This first argument against civil defence has been rejected with the usual amount of derision by Lord Chalfont.[10] He has written that the idea that civil defence 'is in some way provocative is a bizarre hangover from the doctrine of "Mutual Assured Destruction" ' — thereby implying, rather surprisingly, that the doctrine of deterrence has long ago been repudiated. He then goes on to say that

> The suggestion that the protection of one's own people constitutes evidence of aggressive intent is surely one of the more eccentric propositions to surface even in the tortuous world of strategic analysis. That the Soviet Union has never subscribed to it is clearly demonstrated by its own substantial and expensive civil defence arrangements. (It is also of special interest in the context of the unilateralist-neutralist debate that among the most advanced civil defence systems in the world are those in Switzerland and Sweden.)

This passage is a paradigm of bad argument. First, no one has suggested that civil defence constitutes *evidence* of aggressive intentions — only that it is likely to be *perceived* in this way by the enemy. Second, the fact that the Soviet Union is pursuing civil defence would 'demonstrate' that Soviet leaders do not regard it as provocative only if we assume that the Soviet leaders always refrain from being provocative. This assumption is clearly preposterous, and Chalfont himself implicitly rejects it throughout his article. Finally, the only reason that Sweden and Switzerland might be thought to be of 'special interest' is that it is assumed that they point to an inconsistency: for how can British unilateralist-neutralists oppose civil defence when two of their model states (both are neutral and non-nuclear) have vigorous civil defence programmes? But this shows only that Chalfont has missed the force of the argument which he dismisses with so much contempt. The point is that *of course* it is not provocative if Sweden and Switzerland have civil defence, for they do not have nuclear weapons.

But to return to the main line of argument, a second reason why it is bad to cause alarm among the Soviet leaders, and therefore bad to pursue civil defence, is that this strengthens the hand of the hawks inside the Kremlin. Every threatening signal which the West manages to send to the Russians, whether deliberately or inadvertently, helps to substantiate the arguments of the Soviet hawks, thereby adding more fuel to the nuclear arms race. Certainly Russia's own civil defence preparations have been of enormous propaganda value to the hawks in the United States.

Third, in a densely populated country with a high concentration of nuclear weapons on its soil, civil defence is likely to be largely futile. The country would be too heavily hit for most forms of civil defence to be of much use. The only forms which would be of much value would be prohibitively expensive for a country in Britain's economic position. On the other hand, civil defence measures for countries without nuclear weapons may be highly effective. This is because these countries are less likely to be subjected to direct nuclear bombardment, and the fallout which would settle on their territories would be thinner and less intensely radioactive than that which would rain down on the countries in which the explosions had occurred.

Finally, what is most insidious about civil defence preparations is that they can be used to encourage complacence and docility in the population by giving people a false sense of security. By persuading people that they can survive a nuclear war, governments can hope to reduce public opposition to defence planning based on the possible use of nuclear weapons. Of course, if this was part of the Government's intention in issuing 'Protect and Survive', then the scheme has backfired miserably. The publication of that ill-fated document served more to frighten and disillusion people than to soothe them. But this should remind us that another possible effect of civil defence preparations is to foster in people an attitude of

apathetic resignation to the inevitability of nuclear war. This
is no more salutary than an attitude of ignorant complacence.

The public certainly have reason to be suspicious of what
they are told about civil defence and the prospect of surviving a nuclear war by those persons involved in the current
campaign for civil defence. It is revealing that some of these
persons, in planning for the aftermath of a nuclear war, have
urged that the authorities should play down the horrors of
nuclear war, both before and after it occurs, 'in the interests
of morale'. In some cases this amounts to recommending
certain subtle forms of deception. To illustrate the sort of
thing I have in mind, I shall cite a few passages from a recent
book entitled *The Public and the Bomb* by Major-General
Frank M. Richardson.[11]

(a) Richardson quotes from an earlier civil defence pamphlet he wrote, saying that 'many surviving injured cases
who in normal conditions would be priority cases for
admission to hospital, will not be seen by surgeons until
several hours, or even days, after injury.' (p. 27) He later
acknowledges, however, that survivors will have to remain
in their shelters for two weeks or more following a nuclear
attack. (p. 68) Certainly he does not really believe that
doctors will be back in their surgeries awaiting patients
within a few hours after the bomb goes off.

(b) 'You may hear people talk of flash blindness. I am glad
to reassure you that true blindness is very, very rare . . . It
is, therefore, more correct to speak of flash dazzle, and
this will of course pass off before very long, just as it does
if you stare straight into bright sunlight.' (p. 96) It is
interesting to contrast this claim with the fact that in 1958
an American nuclear test burned out the eyes of rabbits
350 miles away from the explosion.[12]

(c) Richardson recommends that, in radio 'broadcast
propaganda' after a nuclear attack, 'it may help to equate
the bomb with ordinary life by comparing flash burn to
sunburn, and radiation sickness to ordinary illness'. (p. 101)
He also suggests that 'those in the worst areas could be
reminded of the Londoners' reaction to the Blitz — "We
can take it" '. (p. 95)

(d) A suggested radio broadcast following a nuclear attack includes the following: 'It is not thought likely that radio-active matter taken into the body — in drinking-water for example — will prove to be a serious threat to health (but in due course people will be examined for such effects, and we would be right to hope that effective methods for removing such matter from our body will before long be developed by our scientists, who have for long been in the forefront in the study of the many problems of ionizing radiation).' (pp. 102-3)

(e) Richardson cites with approval Peter Laurie's view that recovery from a nuclear war would be so rapid that 'in a few decades we might not know that there had been a bomb . . . If [this] estimate of the possibility of recovery seems optimistic, we might remember that a mere two decades after the warring European nations had lost millions of their young men between 1914 and 1918 they were ready to have another go.' (pp. 15-16)

One could go on for pages commenting on these and similar passages with which the book is replete. (There are even passages containing advice on how to dress for the holocaust. Contrary to what Tom Lehrer once suggested, it would not be a 'come as you are' affair.) But the important point is simply that these passages are primarily and transparently intended to soothe and reassure us, and to encourage us to believe that the consequences of nuclear war would not be intolerable. It is possible to see much of the whole civil defence campaign in this light: as an attempt to manipulate our attitude to nuclear war, to encourage us to believe that nuclear war is survivable and therefore acceptable.[13] This, it is thought, will help to weaken public opposition to Britain's nuclear defence policy. There is an amazing passage in 'Protect and Survive' in which it is said that, when the 'all-clear' signal is given, 'this means there is no longer an *immediate* danger from air attack and fall-out and you may resume normal activities'[14] — implying that one will then be free to pick up one's briefcase and hurry off to the office. Nuclear war is presented basically as consisting of two weeks in a cramped shelter with a possibility of injury. (Even the use of the phrase 'air attack' rather than 'nuclear attack' suggests a desire to foster associations between nuclear war and World War II.)

I hope that what has been said is sufficient to show both that there are good reasons for opposing civil defence planning for Britain as long as Britain retains nuclear weapons and that there are good reasons for suspecting the motives of some of those who advocate civil defence but not disarmament. But none of these objections to civil defence, or doubts about the motives of its advocates, would apply if Britain were to renounce the possession of nuclear weapons. There is nothing insidious or destabilizing about civil defence for a country which does not possess nuclear weapons. On the contrary, it is a mere matter of rational prudence.

'Unconventional Defences'

There are various types of unconventional defence arrangements which Britain might adopt. I shall briefly mention two possibilities: territorial defence and civilian resistance. Both of these measures are designed to make a country extremely difficult to occupy and control. If they are combined with maintenance of regular forces, then they would come into play only if the country's conventional forward defences had failed to halt an invasion at the country's borders.

In order to give a brief explanation of the notion of territorial defence, one can do no better than to quote the definition given by Adam Roberts, the foremost authority in Britain on unconventional systems of defence. Roberts writes that

> *Territorial defence* is a system of defence in depth; it is the governmentally-organized defence of a state's own territory. It is aimed at creating a situation in which in invader, even though he may at least for a time gain geographical possession of part or all of the territory, is constantly harassed and attacked from all sides. It is a form of defence strategy which has substantial reliance on a citizen army, including local units of a militia type. Characteristically, a territorial defence system is based on weapons systems,

strategies and methods of military organization which are better suited to their defensive role than to engagements in major military actions abroad.[15]

A system of territorial defence, then, is designed to deter invasion by making the prospect of successfully occupying and ruling a country seem to a potential aggressor very unpromising. It has the advantage, as Roberts points out, of being organized along more purely defensive lines than conventional military structures, and thus poses no offensive threat to potential enemies. It is not, in other words, a provocative form of defence. A further advantage is that it seems to require a more democratic and possibly even a more decentralized military command structure than is possible for a conventional army.

On the other hand, territorial defence has a number of drawbacks. The two most important problems are that it would probably require some form of conscription and would involve at least the partial militarization of British society. Of course, the severity of these problems would depend on how pervasive the system of territorial defence would be. Territorial defence would not have to be all or nothing, but could be implemented to varying degrees. If it were to form only a minor component of Britain's overall system of defence, then many of the tasks it would involve could be carried out by the regular army. Conscription, if required at all, would have to be practiced only on a limited scale, and citizens militias could perhaps be established on a volunteer basis at the local level. (The Ministry of Defence is at present considering a plan to revive the old Home Guard. The plan calls for volunteer recruitment on a local basis. Whitehall's plan differs from the scheme I am envisaging in that the new Home Guard is intended as a supplement to a nuclear-based defence rather than as part of an alternative to it.[16]) On the other hand, if territorial defence were to be a major component in Britain's overall system of defence, then conscription would be required on a large scale, and militarism would become a more dominant element in British culture. In Switzerland, where territorial defence plays a large part in the overall system of defence, all men except conscientious objectors are involved in the citizens militia, and rifles are kept in all households.[17]

A further problem is that British territorial defence would be of no use in the defence of the rest of Western Europe. Since, as we have seen, there are important reasons for Britain to maintain a strong commitment to the collective defence of Western Europe as a whole, there are therefore good reasons for not adopting territorial defence as the dominant component of Britain's overall system of defence. This would be unlikely in any case, since the idea of territorial defence can be expected to meet with considerable opposition from the various service chiefs. This is partly because it is a largely unfamiliar form of defence, and partly because it would serve to erode their authority and would not require the deployment of certain types of weapons systems to which they have grown attached.

On the other hand, while a system of British territorial defence would not actively contribute to the defence of Europe, it would serve to persuade the Russians that the occupation of at least part of Europe would be both difficult and costly. To this extent, then, it would have an indirect deterrent effect against an invasion of Western Europe by the Soviet Union.

The second form of unconventional defence which I shall consider is known as civilian resistance. The idea is that large segments of the civilian population should be trained in techniques of resistance so that, if ever a successful invasion occurs, the occupying power will be met with widespread and coordinated resistance on the part of the population as a whole. The knowledge that he would meet with organized popular resistance might help to dissuade a potential aggressor from ever launching an invasion. In other words, civilian resistance can have a deterrent effect.

Unlike territorial defence, civilian resistance would be largely if not exclusively non-violent. Various possible tactics for civilian resistance have been listed by April Carter, a member of the Alternative Defence Commission. These include:

total non-cooperation through a general strike; selective strikes and boycotts and acts of civil disobedience aimed against particularly objectionable policies; open defiance through mass demonstrations, or passive resistance through industrial going slow, bureaucratic working to rule, and hidden methods of obstruction. Attempts might be made to undermine the morale of troops and officials either by direct argument of the kind used by the Czechs in the early days of the Soviet invasion of 1968, by a social boycott, or by deliberate fraternisation [with the intention of gaining their sympathy].[18]

Civilian resistance, like territorial defence, has the advantage of being purely defensive. It is also a 'safe' form of defence, in the sense that it provides no targets for nuclear attacks. It is certainly inexpensive, and it has the potential for being effective against various types of threat. As Michael Randle has noted, 'the political realism of civilian resistance derives from the fact that no government, and no economic system, can continue to operate without at least the passive co-operation of the population'.[19]

Again, however, civilian resistance is not without its problems. First, it seems to me unrealistic to suppose that civilian resistance could ever form the whole of Britain's system of defence; yet there are problems in trying to couple it with other forms of defence.[20] It may also require a degree of homogeneity in the population which does not at present exist in British society. Finally, the people themselves may find the prospect of resistance training unattractive, though there is reason to hope that people may become sufficiently aware of the dangers of a nuclear-based defence policy that they will be willing to submit to the onerous demands of implementing a safer alternative.

In concluding this survey of the various types of alternative defence which Britain might adopt, I shall briefly suggest how a combination of these types of defence might help to insure against the threat of nuclear blackmail. First, civil defence preparations would be of limited use in deterring nuclear blackmail. The more capable a country is of withstanding the effects of a nuclear attack, the less likely it is to be intimidated by the threat of attack; and the less likely a country is to be intimidated, the less likely it is to be subjected to nuclear blackmail. The most valuable form of civil defence for the purpose of resisting and therefore of deterring nuclear blackmail would be to have large public shelters outside the major cities, along with plans for the evacuation of cities which have been well publicized in advance.

It will be recalled that I earlier mentioned that there are two ways in which the Russians might use nuclear blackmail against Britain. These are to gain the surrender of British troops fighting in Europe, and to gain the surrender of British troops deployed in defence of British territory. Civil defence would help to deter both of these uses of nuclear blackmail. On the other hand, territorial defence and civilian resistance would help to deter only the second of these two uses. They would help to deter this use of nuclear blackmail in the following way. Suppose that the Russians are at the Channel and threaten that, unless Britain surrenders, they will begin bombing British cities. If Britain has a territorial army, and if the British citizenry have been trained in tactics of resistance, then the British government to whom the threat is addressed may not be altogether *capable* of surrendering. As I mentioned earlier, territorial defence may allow for a more decentralized command structure than is possible for a conventional army. Thus it may allow for the deployment of dispersed, relatively autonomous guerrilla units which would have predelegated assignments within particular regions. There is no guarantee that the members of these units would in fact lay down their arms even if the country's leaders were to call for surrender. In a country like Switzerland, where every man of military age has had military training and keeps a gun in his home, an official surrender from the head of state may be next to meaningless. Enemy troops could still expect to meet with armed resistance if they were to attempt to occupy the territory. Remember that territorial defence is defence in depth rather than frontal defence. Thus both it and civilian resistance come into operation only after a country has already been invaded. In this case, the territorial army might wait to attack until the invaders had substantially penetrated British territory. And, once the occupying troops had infiltrated the country, it would then be too late for the Russians to carry out their threatened attacks on British cities — for they would not wish to drop nuclear bombs all over a territory that is filled with their own troops (for example, they would not drop nuclear bombs on Kabul today).

It might also be possible — though this idea may seem crazy — for a country with extensive preparations for territorial defence to make it part of its declared policy that its citizen militiamen are commanded in advance not to surrender, even if, in time of war, the head of state commands them to do so. If it were well known in advance that a country's territorial army would not lay down their arms even if they were instructed to do so, then this would make it largely futile to try to subject such a country to nuclear blackmail. The head of state might agree to surrender, but again this would be a meaningless gesture.

If what I have suggested is right, then, while nuclear blackmail might be effective in gaining the surrender of Britain's forward conventional defences (that is, the forces deployed along the edges of British territory), it would be of less use against a territorial army.

The Soviet Threat

Thus far I have taken it for granted that Britain and the rest of Western Europe face a serious military threat from the Soviet Union and its allies. I have argued on the basis of the assumption that the Soviet Union has reasons for wanting to invade Western Europe, and would in all probability attempt an invasion if it were undeterred from doing so. But, as I mentioned earlier, I have granted this assumption only provisionally. I shall now challenge it.

What evidence is there for the claim that the Soviet Union intends to invade Western Europe if only it is given the opportunity to do so? Two main pieces of evidence are normally adduced here. One is that over the past twenty years the Soviet Union has been remorselessly building up its military strength so that Soviet forces now rival or indeed surpass their American or NATO counterparts in most categories. But, while it is certainly true that the Russians have built up arms on an enormous scale, it is open to question whether this alone indicates that they have aggressive intentions. There are, as Michael Howard has pointed out, a number of possible explanations of the Russians' behaviour:

> atavistic Soviet suspicions of the outside world, the growing collusion of Soviet adversaries East and West, the primacy enjoyed by the military in Soviet bureaucratic processes, a determination to demonstrate super-power status in the only way open to her, above all an understandable determination that any further conflict will be fought out on the soil of her adversaries rather than her own . . .[21]

It should also be mentioned that the intensification of the Soviet arms build-up coincided with the aftermath of the Cuban missile crisis. It was widely held at that time that the Soviet Union had been humiliatingly forced to back down in the Cuban crisis because of its position of nuclear inferiority *vis-à-vis* the US. It is understandable if the Russian leaders vowed at that time never to allow themselves to occupy that position of inferiority again.

Michael Howard's catalogue of possible explanations has been patronizingly dismissed by Lord Chalfont, who claims that 'capabilities and intentions are inseparable'.[22] One wonders if Chalfont has considered the implications of this claim in the case of the US. Throughout the 1950s and early 1960s — indeed until the war in Vietnam began to absorb so much of America's military resources — the US maintained a wide margin of military superiority over the Soviet Union. Did this bespeak an aggressive intent? Does the new administration's avowed aim of restoring superiority bespeak an aggressive intent? Does the fact that the US augments its growing first-strike capability with every new nuclear weapon it acquires necessarily indicate an American intention to launch a first strike? Chalfont writes that 'Soviet military strength is entirely disproportionate to any possible requirement for the territorial defence of the Soviet Union.'[23]

wonder if he is prepared to accept the implications of the fact that this is equally true of the US.

A more persuasive piece of evidence than the mere fact that the Soviet Union has a lot of weapons is that Soviet and Warsaw Pact forces in Europe are clearly structured for offensive manoeuvres. This shows up in a number of ways. For example, the Warsaw Pact has a far higher ratio of tanks (largely offensive weapons) to anti-tank weapons (largely defensive weapons) than NATO does. Warsaw Pact troops also carry antidotes to their own chemical weapons, which suggests that they plan to be moving forward when they use these weapons. The offensive nature of Warsaw Pact strategy also shows up quite clearly in their military exercises and in their strategic doctrine.

Lord Chalfont has claimed that 'any careful examination of the equipment, deployment, tactical doctrines and training methods of the Soviet armed forces seems clearly to establish an aggressive intent'.[24] What is questionable about this view, however, is the assumption that an offensive military posture is necessarily indicative of an aggressive intent. A rival, and to my mind more plausible hypothesis is that the Soviet Union plans for an offensive campaign *in the event of NATO aggression* in order to ensure, as Michael Howard has noted, that the war will be fought 'on the soil of her adversaries'. This hypothesis has been convincingly expounded by Nigel Calder in his book, *Nuclear Nightmares*. There he writes that 'the principle that the best defence is to attack is cardinal at every level of Soviet military thinking'. The Russians aim 'to be able to absorb a sudden act of aggression and quickly roll it back in a counter-attack'. Calder contends that the Russian war plans

add up to a deterrent, no different in principle from the western threat to consume in nuclear fires the men, women and children of Moscow, Leningrad ... and a hundred other Soviet cities. But the Soviet plans contrast so sharply in style with the western ideas of deterrence that it is hard to recognise them for what they are.[25]

In opposition to the view that the Soviet Union would like to take over Western Europe, Robert Neild has argued that the Russians actually have no interest in trying to do so:

> I can think of no worse disaster for the Soviet Union than to be landed with more revolting colonies in Europe. On the contrary, she is an over-extended empire on the defensive.[26]

But, even if the Soviet Union did desire to absorb Western Europe into its empire, it is highly questionable whether it could muster the manpower necessary to carry out a successful invasion. One reason for this is of course that the Red Army is already heavily taxed with having to maintain troops all along the Sino-Soviet border as well as in Afghanistan. It is already stretched so thin that it could not itself mount an invasion of Western Europe without leaving the Soviet Union exposed to attack from other quarters. Nor can the Soviet leaders afford to count on the support of the other Warsaw Pact armies. Robin Cook and Dan Smith have made the following observations about the cohesion of the Warsaw Pact:

> The USSR's lack of confidence in the alliance is eloquently revealed by the concentration of virtually the entire Pact armaments industry within the Soviet Union and by the relatively older equipment which it makes available to its allies. US intelligence headquarters in Stuttgart review weekly the reliability of the Soviet allies; their general conclusion is that these allies would be reliable in the event of a NATO invasion, but would be unlikely to support Soviet aggression.[27]

It is important to remember that the Warsaw Pact armies are composed largely of conscripts. It is not at all improbable that, in the event of an aggressive Soviet campaign, many of the Warsaw Pact armies would fight *against* the Soviet army rather than alongside it.

Both the 1980 and 1981 *Statements of Defence Estimates* concede that there is no reason to believe that the Soviet

leaders are deliberately planning to attack NATO. What I
have argued thus far supports the stronger conclusion that
they would not be planning to attack NATO even if NATO
were less prepared than it is to respond to an attack.

At this point it is, regrettably, necessary to repudiate a
charge which is increasingly being urged against those who
question the orthodox view that the Soviet Union is poised
to attack the moment NATO lets down its guard — or indeed
those who question *any* of the fundamental assumptions of
Britain's current defence policy. This is the charge of pro-
Sovietism. There is at present an ugly smear campaign being
mounted by certain persons on the right which attempts to
portray the disarmament movement in Britain as a communist-
inspired conspiracy. Hence Lord Chalfont: 'it has to be said
that a *considerable number* of those who advocate unilateral
disarmament do so because they wish to see this country
defenceless against the designs of the Soviet Union'.[28] I trust
that this sort of slander will be seen as discrediting only to
those who indulge in it. There is of course a handful of
people in this country who would welcome a Soviet victory
over the West, and of course these people favour unilateral
disarmament. They believe, basically, that Britain's missiles
are aimed in the wrong direction. But to try to establish an
association between these people and the disarmament movement as a whole is no fairer than it would be to try to foster
an association between persons like Lord Chalfont and certain fanatical right-wing militarist groups who happen to
share his attachment to nuclear weapons.

Finally, in concluding this section, a word needs to be said
about why even non-nuclear defences are needed if the orthodox vision of the Soviet threat to Europe is largely fictitious.
If in fact the Soviet threat is as improbable as I have suggested, then what is there for Britain to defend against?

First, and most important, my assessment of the Soviet
threat is only of the *immediate* threat. No one can say that
there will be no Soviet threat in the future. (There was no
apparent German threat before Hitler embarked on rearmament. In 1932, the German army was very small and had
only a relatively tiny number of tanks. But Europe was soon
to be faced with an enormous German threat.) The present

Soviet leadership will not last forever, and no one can predict what their successors' attitudes towards Western Europe will be. Prudence requires that we should make some preparations for the possibility that there will some day be a serious Soviet threat.

Second, judgements about people's intentions are never incorrigible. This is especially true when the people in question happen to be the members of a government whose deliberations are highly secretive and whose public pronouncements are not known for their honesty and candour. So it would be unwise to attribute too much weight to my admittedly fallible speculations about Soviet intentions with regard to Europe — especially when what is at stake is national survival.

Finally, there is the simple fact that most people would find it unacceptable to live in a country which lacked defences. We are accustomed to having a strong national army, and would feel exposed and vulnerable in its absence. This is perhaps not in itself a particularly important reason for having defences, but it is vitally important that the disarmament movement, if it hopes to succeed, should take account of the fact that this attitude exists. For nuclear disarmament will not be a goal acceptable to most people unless it is accompanied by proposals for filling the gap left by the abandonment of nuclear weapons. The disarmament campaign must demonstrate to people that unilateralism has a positive as well as a negative aspect; otherwise it will be received by many as a counsel of despair. A correspondent to *The Times*, quoted with approval by Lord Hill-Norton, has claimed that 'at the centre of the Campaign for Nuclear Disarmament there is hopelessness, thinly disguised as "concern" and mobilized as protest'.[29] How anyone could honestly believe that hopelessness is the motivating force behind the most dynamic and burgeoning mass movement of our time is somewhat hard to understand; but this particular piece of propaganda may nevertheless gain ground if CND allows itself to be portrayed as being simply *against* nuclear weapons and not *for* anything. If CND is to succeed then it must present itself as being, not against defence but in favour of *rational* defence.

CND is, of course, not opposed to defence for Britain. In a

letter to *The Times*, Monsignor Bruce Kent, the General Secretary of CND, has written that 'the way forward, which at least offers some hope, must lie in the exploration of alternative defence policies, military and non-military . . .'[30] Yet only three days before Kent's letter appeared, a leader column in *The Guardian* claimed that CND 'offers to leave Britain (or in other contexts, Western Europe) effectively defenceless . . .'[31] The fact that the writer of this column seems quite sympathetic to CND shows just how pervasive is the illusion that CND opposes defence.

The Economic Argument

The second argument concerns the economic costs of maintaining a nuclear force. The basic claim is simply that nuclear weapons consume financial resources which would be better allocated to other, more worthy projects. This claim is clearly linked with the first argument for abandoning nuclear weapons since, if non-nuclear defences would be more rational for Britain, then defence spending should be devoted to building up defences of this sort rather than to the maintenance of nuclear forces. It is often claimed, moreover, that there are two other main areas in which public funds would be better spent: namely, domestic social services and non-military foreign aid.

This economic argument is directed primarily at such costly projects as *Trident*. It counts much less against the proposed cruise missiles, the cost of which will be borne largely by the US. (The cost to Britain of the entire 'modernization' programme involving cruise missiles and *Pershing II*s will be about £16 million.[32]) The argument scarcely touches the American forward-based systems, since, as far as I know, these cost Britain very little.

Consider first the impact which such projects as *Trident* are having on Britain's conventional forces. Not only are they preventing an increase in spending on conventional and unconventional defences, but they are actually necessitating reductions in Britain's conventional forces. The projected cost of *Trident* was originally set at £5 billion. It has since escalated to £6 billion. That works out to a little under £500 for every family in Britain, and experience suggests that the actual costs will eventually prove to be even higher.[33] In order to meet these costs, the Defence Secretary will have to make drastic cuts in Britain's conventional forces — the main target probably being the Royal Navy.

I wrote earlier that Britain's European allies might prefer Britain to increase its conventional forces rather than maintain its independent deterrent. It certainly seems to be true that they would prefer Britain to maintain its present conventional forces rather than sacrifice them for the sake of *Trident*. There is growing and undisguised concern within NATO over Britain's decision to purchase *Trident* at the expense of its conventional forces. And there is certainly good reason for the NATO allies to be alarmed. Certain reductions in Britain's forces may leave important gaps in NATO's defences that no other NATO countries will be able to fill. For example, a major task of the Royal Navy is the defence of the North Atlantic, including the Iceland Gap, through which US ships bearing supplies and reinforcements must pass on their way to Northern Europe. Leaving this area undefended might mean that fewer supplies would get through to NATO's conventional forces in the course of a European war, thereby forcing an early escalation to the nuclear level.

NATO is already dangerously over-reliant on nuclear weapons. Even defenders of nuclear weapons concede that these must be supplemented by strong conventional forces. Otherwise they lose whatever credibility they might have as a deterrent. American strategists, for example, realized long ago that their strategic nuclear weapons could not deter acts of limited conventional aggression by a nuclear-armed adversary. Similarly, the deterrent value for Europe of NATO's nuclear forces will be seriously eroded unless these forces are underpinned by a strong conventional capacity.

A problem which must at this point be admitted is that an alternative, non-nuclear defence policy for Britain might end up costing more than a policy with a substantial nuclear component. This is clearly possible. After all, one of the major reasons why TNW were first deployed in Europe was that they were cheaper than maintaining high conventional force levels. But, if an adequate non-nuclear defence would in fact be more costly than the present mixed system of defence, this will be very bad news for those whose opposition to nuclear weapons stems in part from a desire to see the money being spent on nuclear weapons spent instead on welfare programmes at home and the relief of poverty in the Third World.

The moral case for doing more to relieve the suffering of needy people in developing countries seems to me over-whelming.[34] A much less important reason for spending more on foreign aid, but one which is particularly relevant to the concerns of this book, is that it could serve to check Soviet expansionism by removing certain sources of political unrest in Third World countries which the Soviet Union might try to exploit to its advantage. There may even be reason to believe that increased foreign aid expenditure would gain more respect for the West than it currently enjoys in many Third World countries. Increasing foreign aid is therefore an aim which it would be rational for opponents of Soviet expansionism to support; but they seem not to have noticed this. (Early in 1981 the Director of the US Office of Management and Budget proposed severe cuts in *non-military* foreign aid — primarily so that the money could be channelled into the defence budget.)

Comparisons are often drawn between Britain and countries like Sweden and Switzerland which maintain strong non-nuclear defences. These comparisons are often intended to show that non-nuclear defences for Britain would be more expensive, but it is doubtful whether they are in fact very illuminating. For example, it is often noted that Sweden spends more *per capita* on defence than Britain, but it is less often mentioned that Britain spends a considerably greater proportion of its GNP on defence than Sweden.

I am myself optimistic about the possibility of construct-ing adequate non-nuclear defences at a lower cost than the present policy imposes; but, since I have no expertise in this area, I shall not offer this optimism in the form of a judge-ment. Britain should clearly do what will increase its chances of national survival, but a point may eventually be reached where defence needs may have to be traded off against social needs and the need to eliminate poverty and hunger in the Third World.

The Prudential Argument

I have already given reasons for thinking that a Warsaw Pact invasion of Western Europe is unlikely. The likely causes of war are, it seems, for the most part external to Europe (unless, of course, we include wars to suppress colonial rebellions within Eastern Europe). Nevertheless, if a super-power war were to break out, even for reasons wholly uncon-nected with Europe, Britain and certain other NATO states in Western Europe would be ineluctably caught up in the conflagration. The reason for this is connected with the presence of nuclear weapons and certain strategic support systems on West European soil. As was mentioned earlier, these are prime targets for preemptive strikes. It is therefore an argument against having nuclear weapons that their possession is sufficient for making Britain the target of large-scale nuclear attacks in the event of a war between the superpowers.

Britain and Western Europe might even be the *first* casualties in a war between the US and the USSR. Paul Warnke, former director of the US Arms Control and Disarmament Agency under President Carter, has claimed that,

If the Soviets ever feel they have to start a nuclear war I think the first thing they would do would be to wipe out any of the theatre nuclear forces that are stationed in Western Europe. They think that would be the least provocative thing they could do in terms of the United States.[35]

Priority targets for Soviet nuclear attacks would obviously be those nuclear weapons systems capable of striking within the Soviet Union and those strategic support facilities which make a vital contribution to the ability of the US to wage a strategic nuclear war. Thus cruise missile sites, and the areas in which the cruise missiles would be dispersed, would be prominent targets.[36] So would such facilities as the submarine tracking station at Brawdy and the Fylingdales Early Warning System. Britain's submarines at sea would not be targets whose destruction would threaten urban populations, but the ports which they use and stations used to communicate with them would. US air bases in Britain where F-111s are stationed and where nuclear weapons are stored would also be important targets. The prudential argument counts against all of these.

The official view of the Government is that the presence of nuclear weapons on British soil does not make a nuclear attack on Britain more likely. Here are a few quotations which illustrate the Government's position on the issue.

(a) In this year's *Statement of Defence Estimates*, there is a popular essay entitled 'Nuclear Weapons and Preventing War' in which it is asserted that 'whether we like the fact or not, and whether nuclear weapons are based here or not, our country's size and location make it militarily crucial to NATO and so an inevitable target in war. A "nuclear free" Britain would mean [that] if a war started we would if anything be more likely, not less, to come under nuclear attack.'[37]

(b) Mr Geoffrey Pattie, the Undersecretary of Defence for the RAF, stated before the House of Commons that 'Unilateralists argue that [nuclear disarmament] would make Britain less of a nuclear target, but Russia could not ignore a country of such obvious political and strategic importance. No NATO member could expect to be exempt from any nuclear conflict.'[38]

(c) Finally, I have in my possession a letter written on behalf of the Secretary of Defence by one of his private secretaries in which an attempt is made to explain Government policy on nuclear weapons. Here it is stated that 'it is an unfortunate fact that the geographic, industrial and political importance of the United Kingdom has always meant that it would be a prime target in any attack upon the West. The presence or absence of nuclear weapons on British soil makes no difference.'

The reader will note that these explanations of why the presence of nuclear weapons does not make Britain more likely to be attacked are conspicuous for their lack of specificity. There are vague references to Britain's size and location and its great importance in several respects, but no attempt is made to show how these factors make Britain a target for nuclear attacks. Are we to suppose that the Russians will attack all countries which are of Britain's size, or which are in some vague way of political importance? The best reason I can think of for supposing that Britain would still be subject to nuclear attack if it did not have nuclear weapons is that the Russians would want to destroy certain potential staging posts for American reinforcements on their way to Central Europe. But even if we grant this, it remains true that, if Britain did not have nuclear weapons, it would surely be attacked less heavily. The Russians will not be tempted to drop bombs where Britain's nuclear weapons and support facilities *used* to be. Can the government explain to the residents of Brawdy, for example, why *they* would be just as likely to be hit even if the station for tracking Russian submarines were removed?

Lord Chalfont has also attacked the prudential argument, claiming that 'it is an obscure argument, since the British nuclear striking force is largely submarine based'.[39] One wonders how much comfort the residents of Upper Heyford, Lakenheath, Rugby, Greenham Common, etc. will derive from this observation.

The urgency of the prudential argument derives from the fact that a war between the superpowers is becoming increasingly probable. But before going on to discuss some of the reasons why war is becoming more likely, I shall briefly discuss the possibility of what is known as 'limited nuclear war' and show how this is related to the prudental argument for abandoning nuclear weapons.

Nuclear war might be 'limited' in either of two ways. It might be limited in the sense that relatively few bombs would go off, so that the destruction would be less than total. Or it might be limited in the sense of being confined to a certain geographical area, or theatre of war. It is this second form of limited nuclear war which I shall discuss, and the particular theatre I shall be concerned with is Europe. There is now a growing fear in Europe that, if war breaks out between the superpowers, then, regardless of where the war breaks out or what its cause is, it will be fought using Europe as the battlefield. The homelands of the superpowers will, by tacit agreement, be preserved as sanctuaries. This scenario was suggested long ago by General de Gaulle:

> Who can say that if the occasion arises the two [superpowers], while each deciding not to launch its missiles at the main enemy so that it should itself be spared, will not crush the others? It is possible to imagine that on some awful day Western Europe should be wiped out from Moscow and Central Europe from Washington. And who can say that the two rivals, after I know not what political and social upheaval, will not unite?[40]

Only the ending of this scenario now sounds fanciful. Ironically, limited nuclear war in Europe is made possible by the very weapons which were originally intended to guarantee the 'coupling' of European and American security. When the Soviet Union first acquired nuclear weapons, it was thought to be no longer credible for the US to threaten to use its strategic nuclear forces in the event of a conventional attack on Western Europe. So, to make the threat of retaliation more credible, theatre nuclear weapons were installed in order to provide a ladder of escalation from conventional to strategic nuclear war. (See the earlier discussion of the first version of the trigger argument.) But once they were installed, it then became possible to fight a nuclear war using theatre weapons only. Clearly, the superpowers both have the strongest imaginable incentive to limit a war fought with TNW to the area of the theatre.

Only recently it has been revealed that the Pentagon has asked that all the major hospitals in the US should keep a certain proportion of their beds free at all times in order to be able to receive wounded servicemen during or after a nuclear war in Europe. Anthony Tucker, who has reported this fact in *The Guardian*, rightly points out that this 'policy confirms . . . the American belief that the US mainland will not be attacked'.[41] This alarming new development should make us aware of just how serious the US is in its intention to use Europe as the battlefield for its war with the Soviet Union.

It is also important to notice how profoundly destabilizing this trend in American strategic thinking is. It is always easier to decide to go to war if you believe that the war can be fought on someone else's territory, leaving your own territory exempt from the carnage. Thus, insofar as the US believes that it could fight a nuclear war confined to Europe, it will be to that extent less inhibited about fighting a nuclear war.

The link between the possibility of limited nuclear war and the prudential argument is obvious: for the superpowers cannot use Europe as their nuclear battlefield unless there are nuclear weapons there to fight it with. Moreover, the alleged Russian need to strike preemptively at nuclear weapons stationed in Europe would provide an ideal excuse to transport to Europe a war which had broken out elsewhere (for example, in the Middle East, where an American rapid deployment force might be engaged in conventional combat against Soviet troops).

(It should be mentioned here, in fairness to the advocates of nuclear weapons, that the British and French independent strategic forces constitute an obstacle, from the Soviet point of view, to keeping a European war limited. Since these weapons are capable of hitting targets within the Soviet Union, the Russians have less reason than the Americans to hope that their territory could remain a sanctuary.[42] Thus these weapons may help to deter both superpowers from thinking that they could escape unscathed from a war in Europe. (If the Russians were attacked, they would in all probability attack the US in order to prevent the US from having an advantage.) But since, as I have argued, the threat to use small forces independently in the event of an invasion is only doubtfully credible, and is therefore of questionable deterrent value, it seems to me that a better way of preventing limited nuclear war in Europe would be to try to remove as many nuclear weapons from European territory as possible.)

In order to substantiate the earlier claim, on which the prudential argument is based, that war between the super-powers is far more likely than a war of European origin, I shall now briefly cite some of the ways in which superpower deterrence might break down. Perhaps the most ominous of all the recent trends is the increasing ability of both the US and the Soviet Union to launch a disabling first strike against the other side's retaliatory forces. I explained earlier in the first section of Chapter II why the temptation to strike first against the other side's forces is so strong: it would almost infallibly give the aggressor the advantage, and might even allow him to emerge victorious without having suffered a single strike against his own territory. It should also be clear why this possibility is so dangerously destabilizing. If one side has a greater first-strike capability than the other, and both know this, then the side with the greater capability may be tempted to seize the opportunity to strike while the opportunity presents itself. But the other side, knowing that it is at a disadvantage, will then feel tempted to strike first itself in order to avoid being defeated. Realizing that the weaker side is thinking this way, the stronger side will feel all the more urgently pressured to attack. With both sides caught up in this vicious circle, restraint may eventually come to seem suicidal.

The American strategic analyst Herman Kahn has recently predicted that nuclear war is more likely to occur during the next three or four years than at any other time until the end of the century.[43] The reasoning behind this prediction is that the Russians will enjoy strategic superiority over the US until some time around the middle of the decade, at which time the US will regain superiority and will continue to maintain it. Thus the Russians realize that, if they ever hope to win a nuclear war by conducting a first strike, it is now or never. And the Americans know that the Russians understand this.

The situation is roughly the same if both sides have an equal capability for launching a disabling first strike. This phenomenon is known as 'symmetrical destabilization'. If each side has the capacity largely to disarm the other, there will be a high premium on striking first, and each side's forces will be on a hair-trigger in times of tension. Indeed, the very possibility of a first strike by either side serves to aggravate tensions and heighten fears on all sides, thereby impelling both sides towards a war which both would prefer to avoid. Each will be pressured to strike first, not so much by a desire to defeat or destroy the other, but by the fear of being defeated or destroyed itself.

There are numerous factors leading to the development of a greater first-strike capability by both sides. One is the increasing tendency on both sides to add MIRVs, or a greater number of MIRVs, to their missiles. Suppose that each side has ten warheads on each missile. By aiming two warheads at each of the other side's missile silos, an aggressor can hope to destroy *fifty* of his opponent's warheads with a single missile. This is a very advantageous trade from the point of view of the aggressor.

Another factor is that each side is currently developing increasingly accurate missiles. This is very important. The probability of one missile being able to destroy another missile in its silo is a function both of the first missile's accuracy and of the explosive power of its warhead, but accuracy is more important than explosive power. Professor Michael Pentz has calculated that, if you increase the power of a bomb by a factor of ten (that is, tenfold), you increase the probability that it will destroy its target (a missile in its silo) by only about four and a half times; whereas if you improve the accuracy by a factor of ten, you increase this probability 100-fold. Pentz concludes that, 'if what you are after is increased *counterforce* capacity, you should concentrate first and foremost on greater accuracy'.[44]

The trend towards greater accuracy in nuclear weapons has come about partly in order to meet the requirements of certain strategic doctrines, such as America's 'countervailing strategy' recently set forth by President Carter in Presidential Directive 59. But one suspects that new doctrines have been devised in part in order to accommodate the new, more accurate weapons, and find a use for them. More accurate weapons have probably been developed mainly as a result of the inner logic of scientific research: once the scientists have invented certain weapons, it is difficult to prevent them from 'improving' these weapons by making them more accurate.

Other factors which contribute to the development of a first-strike capability are civil defence, the development and deployment of ABM systems, and advances in ASW technology. Civil defence and ABM systems would help to shield the aggressor against any possible retaliation after a first strike, and ASW would be an essential component of a successful first strike. As we have seen, both the US and the Soviet Union are pursuing vigorous programmes in all three of these areas, though the US is lagging behind in the area of civil defence.

In short, both the US and the USSR seem to be doing everything possible to destabilize the balance of power.

There are a variety of other ways in which superpower deterrence might break down. One is that, in the course of their global competition for control of resources, economic markets, etc., the superpowers might meet in conventional combat, which would then escalate to the nuclear level. This could happen in the course of their competition for control of the oil fields around the Persian Gulf.

Another source of danger lies in the spread of nuclear weapons to more and more countries. This is known as 'horizontal proliferation'. I have already mentioned that India is preparing for a nuclear explosive test which will probably have occurred by the time this book is published. Pakistan has also been furtively pursuing the development of nuclear weapons, and there are indications that it too is preparing to test a nuclear explosive.[45] It is also suspected (with a high degree of confidence) that both Israel and South Africa already have nuclear weapons. And many other countries — such as Iraq, Brazil and Argentina — may have them fairly soon.[46] This means that there will soon be a possibility of regional nuclear wars in which the superpowers, because of their commitments to the warring countries and their interests in the region, may become embroiled.

Finally, there is always the possibility of an unpremeditated nuclear war. This could come about 'as a result of accident ... misinterpretation of orders, ineffective command and control procedures, nuclear terrorism, or sheer madness'.[47]

Of these, accidental nuclear war is probably the most likely. There are three main ways in which a war might start by accident. One is through the accidental detonation of a nuclear bomb. This is, however, an unlikely cause of war. First, although there have been a great many major accidents involving nuclear weapons, there has never been an instance in which a nuclear weapon has actually exploded, and the probability of one doing so is slight.[48] And even if one were to go off, the probability is small that this would be misinterpreted as an enemy attack, thereby prompting 'retaliation'. What is more worrying is the possibility that war will occur as the result of the accidental or unauthorized firing of one of one side's weapons against the other side.[49] And what is perhaps most worrying of all is the possibility of a war starting as the result of a false warning of a nuclear attack. A false alarm could lead to war in a number of ways. The most obvious is of course that one side, on receiving a false signal and not discovering the error in time, would launch its missiles on warning or in 'retaliation'. Another possibility is that, on receiving a false signal, one side might go to a high level of alert. Perceiving this, but not knowing the cause, the other side might become fearful that it was about to be attacked, and so place its forces on a high level of alert. This in turn might serve to confirm the suspicions of the first side, and so on until one side would eventually feel compelled to launch.

What makes this the most worrying of the three possible sources of an accidental nuclear war is that false alarms seem to be a fairly regular occurrence. There have recently been two major false alarms in the US which received considerable publicity. In one, which occurred in November 1979, a technician fed a war game tape into a computer while inadvertently failing to identify the tape to the computer as a mere simulation.[50] In the other, in June 1980, a faulty chip in a communications device caused the device to signal that a nuclear attack had occurred. (This same chip later failed again, generating another false signal; but this time it was expected that this might happen.) In both of these cases, B-52 bomber crews and ICBM control units moved to a state of 'nuclear war alert'.

A congressional report released in October 1980 has revealed that the problem is far more serious than most of us ever suspected. The report has disclosed that the North American Air Defence Command (NORAD) experienced 147 serious false alarms over the period between 30 December 1978 and 30 June 1980. This comes to an average of over two per week. In one incident, a radar station in Oregon picked up 'a low orbit rocket body that was close to decay and generated a false launch and impact report'.[51] What this means is that the radar detected a rocket body which was dropping from space and interpreted it as an incoming Soviet missile. It even reported that the 'missile' had 'impacted'. The report also disclosed that over the same eighteen-month period there were an additional 3,703 minor false alarms

caused when the infrared sensors in satellites over the Soviet Union picked up from the earth's surface or the atmosphere indications other than those from a missile. They included fuel-tank explosions, airplane crashes, forest fires, sun flares, and similar atmospheric disturbances.[52]

The report just cited also quotes Air Force officials as saying that equipment failures cause false alarms as serious as those in November 1979 and June 1980 two or three times every year. More recently, an unpublished report drawn up by the General Accounting Office, an investigative body attached to the US Congress, has revealed that some part of the US defence communications network and nuclear early warning system has failed during every military crisis throughout the 1970s.[53] The head of the General Accounting Office has told a subcommittee of the House of Representatives that the US's computer warning system has been outmoded for years. At the same time that this report was concluded, a Republican Congressman conceded that false alarms caused by defects in the system could cause a nuclear war.

The only information we have about false alarms comes from the US, and the fact that much of this information is disclosed only belatedly suggests that more has happened than has been revealed to the public. Also, unless we suppose that the Russians have vastly better equipment than the US (a completely implausible assumption), then we must assume that they too have experienced numerous false alarms.

Unless there is a dramatic reversal in the present course of events, it is difficult to see how war between the superpowers can be avoided. If Britain wishes to prepare prudently for this eventuality, it should remove as many potential targets from its soil as possible. Nuclear weapons on British soil cannot prevent a superpower war from occurring, and, if such a war does occur, they are far more likely to invite nuclear attacks against Britain than to deter them.

The Dangers of Retaliatory Deterrence

We have seen that the point of Britain's having an independent nuclear force is that Britain will then be able to attempt to deter various forms of aggression through the threat of retaliation. I have suggested, however, that it may be more reasonable for Britain to abandon retaliatory deterrence in favour of an alternative defence policy which aims to deter aggression solely by defensive means. (As I mentioned, it will not be possible to arrive at an informed judgement on this issue until we have completed our survey of the arguments against nuclear weapons.) But it should be conceded that some forms of aggression can probably be more effectively deterred by the threat of retaliation than by the threat of 'gain denial'. Nuclear blackmail is a case in point. While I have suggested that certain defensive measures may help to deter one use of nuclear blackmail, it nevertheless seems very improbable that the use of nuclear blackmail to gain the surrender of conventional forces in Europe can be effectively deterred except by the threat of retaliation. This constitutes a strong argument for maintaining a retaliatory capability — though I have argued that Britain ought not to expend its limited resources to maintain such a capability as long as the US has one.

It will be recalled, however, that I also pointed out that the consequences of retaliatory deterrence failing against nuclear blackmail could be appalling. If deterrence fails and Britain does not surrender, then this could lead to a series of strikes and counterstrikes against British and Russian cities which would leave many millions of people dead. This would not be the case if defensive deterrence against nuclear blackmail were to fail. Consider territorial defence and civilian resistance as a deterrent against nuclear blackmail. (See pp. 83-85.) If this form of deterrence were to fail, and the blackmail threat were to be issued, then the rational thing for Britain's leaders to do would be to surrender. (Remember that this would not mean that the people would simply have to submit to Soviet rule. Armed and unarmed resistance would commence as soon as the occupying army became dispersed throughout the country.) There would be no strikes and counterstrikes against cities. So, while the threat of retaliation is likely to be a more effective deterrent against this particular use of nuclear blackmail, it is also a far more dangerous one.

If this point can be generalized, then it will provide another argument against Britain's having an independent nuclear deterrent. The argument, stated simply, is that the possession of nuclear weapons for purposes of deterrence is dangerous because, if deterrence fails, the consequences are likely to be unimaginably horrible. Of course, this may not be a strong objection if there is no alternative to relying on retaliatory deterrence. (For example, there is presumably no adequate deterrent against the total nuclear destruction of a country except the threat of retaliation.) But, when a defensive alternative is available, this may be preferable since, even though it may be a less effective deterrent, it will normally be a far safer one.

Now there are some instances in which defensive measures may be a more effective deterrent than the threat of retaliation. A conventional invasion of Western Europe, for example, would be better deterred by stronger conventional forces than by the threat to retaliate, since the threat is in this case simply not credible. Yet there are other cases, such as nuclear blackmail in Europe, in which the threat to retaliate would be more likely to succeed. But in all cases the threat to retaliate carries greater risks than those which go along with defensive deterrence. The fear is that, even if retaliatory deterrence is on balance more likely to be effective, the

— dif threats

greater risks involved in relying on retaliatory rather than defensive deterrence may outweigh this benefit.

Let us consider a particular example in which this problem emerges vividly. Suppose that Russian forces have swept across Europe and have now reached the Channel. In this situation, would we prefer Britain to have an independent nuclear force or an entrenched territorial army? An independent nuclear force might be more likely to deter the Russians from attempting to occupy the country. Britain's leaders might threaten to begin destroying Russian cities if the Russian forces begin to cross the Channel. Perhaps this would work; but if it did not the consequences might be disastrous. If the Russians were not deterred, and Britain's leaders did not back down on their threat, this would almost inevitably lead to a series of strikes and counterstrikes against British and Russian cities. If Britain were forced to surrender after the mutual slaughter had begun, this would be far worse than if Britain had simply surrendered in the first place. (I admit that this depends on how one evaluates the destruction of Britain as compared with Britain's falling under Soviet domination. I shall return to this later.) And even if Britain were to prevail, this might end up being worse than an initial surrender would have been. Britain might prevail only because it would become so badly damaged that the Russians would cease to have an interest in it. If, on the other hand, Britain were to have a territorial army rather than an independent nuclear force, this might be a less effective deterrent, but the failure of this deterrent would have far less serious consequences. The failure of deterrence in this case would lead to a partly conventional partly unconventional war on British territory. The consequences of such a war would almost certainly be less disastrous than the wholesale destruction of British cities with nuclear bombs.

This example is intended only to clarify the nature of the argument. The general point of the argument is that, even if we decide that, on balance, a retaliatory capability provides a more effective deterrent against the range of threats which Britain faces, we must nevertheless take into account the fact that this form of deterrence carries greater risks than other, perhaps less effective forms of deterrence. In the end we must balance the benefits derived from having a more effective deterrent against the potential costs involved in having a more dangerous one.

Against Cruise Missiles

Thus far I have devoted considerable space to arguments which are primarily concerned with whether or not Britain should have an *independent* retaliatory capability. These arguments are relevant to the debate over *Trident*. Cruise missiles, which also provide a retaliatory capability, though not an independent one, have received comparatively little attention. I shall now attempt to remedy this deficiency by briefly discussing the deterrent value of cruise missiles.[54]

Earlier I gave three reasons for doubting the deterrent value of Britain's SLBM force. These were: (a) that the actual use of the force would in many if not most instances seem to be irrational, (b) that the force may become vulnerable to preemption, and (c) that the Russians may erect defences against it. It can be argued that there are similar reasons for doubting the deterrent value of the proposed cruise missiles.

First, remember that the cruise missiles will be controlled exclusively by the US, and that the use of these missiles against the Soviet Union would bring retaliation against the US just as surely as the use of American-based missiles would. There is, therefore, no reason to believe that these would be more likely to be used in the course of a European war than weapons based in the US. The stationing of cruise missiles in Europe will not increase deterrence in Europe any more than a comparable addition to the US-based strategic arsenal would. In other words, it is unlikely that they will significantly enhance deterrence in Europe.

Second, there are good grounds for thinking that the cruise missiles will be vulnerable to preemptive strikes — even though they will be mounted on mobile launching platforms (namely, lorries) and thus may be dispersed throughout parts of the country in times of international tension. Notice, first, that the possibility of dispersal provides insurance against preemption only when there are indications that war is imminent. A *surprise* first strike could easily destroy all the cruise missiles at their bases. There are, moreover, good reasons for refraining from dispersing the cruise missiles during times of crisis. The dispersal of the cruise missiles would contribute to what is known as 'crisis instability'. The Russians would immediately be alerted (by spies if necessary) when the cruise missiles would begin to be dispersed. And they would be likely to interpret the dispersal as an indication that the US was preparing for war. This would clearly serve to heighten tensions and therefore to increase the likelihood of war. It was because the West was afraid of unduly alarming the Soviet leaders in this way that civil defence plans were not executed in the US or Britain during the Cuban missile crisis. One can only hope that, when we next approach the brink, our leaders will take similarly prudent steps — including refraining from dispersing European cruise missiles (if they are here). Yet, if the cruise missiles are not dispersed, they will be highly vulnerable if war breaks out.

If the cruise missiles are dispersed, will this guarantee them immunity to preemption? It would certainly help to reduce the threat of preemption, but it would nevertheless not eliminate it altogether. A recent US government study concedes that the Russians could know by means of 'covert intelligence' the general location of many of the lorries bearing the cruise missiles. This means that, by conducting air-burst saturation attacks with very large bombs over the areas where the missiles are suspected of being, the Russians could hope, if not to destroy the missiles altogether, at least to disrupt their navigational systems, thereby rendering them ineffective. This should be a rather sobering reflection for persons living in areas to which the missiles might be taken — that is, for people living in the southeast of England.

Finally, given that the US plans to invest heavily in a large force of air-launched cruise missiles, it is reasonable to expect that the Soviet Union will soon be setting up large-scale defences against attacks by cruise missiles. Britain's experience of defending against V-1 attacks in World War II suggests that relatively effective defences against cruise missiles should be possible.[55] These are not banned by any international treaty or agreement. I argued earlier that European-based cruise missiles would probably be used only in conjunction with US-based strategic forces in the course of a general nuclear war. In this case the defences would presumably be saturated, and a fair proportion of the European-based missiles would be able to penetrate to their targets. But the fact that they could penetrate as part of a large-scale *American* attack is of little relevance to the security of *Europe*. On the other hand, if the European-based missiles were to be used independently of the American air-launched cruise missile force, then a much smaller proportion could be expected to penetrate. As Jonathan Alford notes, 'Soviet defences erected against the expectation of a massive American attack of some thousands of missiles could effect a much higher rate of attrition against a smaller force.'[56]

Even if Soviet defences against cruise missiles prove less effective than is anticipated, there is already good reason to suspect that the cruise missiles themselves will be less effective than they have been expected to be. Tests thus far have revealed many flaws in the performance of cruise missiles, and yet these tests have been carried out under highly favourable conditions — conditions much more favourable than those which would exist if the missiles were ever used against the Soviet Union. For example, cruise missiles perform best over hilly terrain, but most of the European and Soviet territory over which they would have to fly in wartime is significantly flatter than the territory in the US over which they have been tested. Moreover, the US has been able to supply the cruise missiles with accurate and detailed maps of the US terrain over which they have been tested. But maps of Soviet and Eastern European territory have to be obtained by satellites and thus are of a much poorer quality. A major problem which has yet to be solved is that cruise missiles would be largely useless against the Soviet Union in winter when many of the distinctive features of the Soviet landscape, such as rivers and lakes, would be obscured by snow.

The foregoing arguments all lead to the conclusion that cruise missiles will not significantly enhance deterrence in Europe. They may well, however, attract blanket attacks with nuclear weapons over large areas of England. They are, as I shall argue in the next section, provocative. Finally, they are potentially destabilizing. They are highly accurate (when they work) and are thus capable of destroying targets, such as Soviet missile silos. They are, in short, 'war-fighting' weapons. Of course, it is true (contrary to a popular misconception) that cruise missiles are not ideally suited for a first-strike role. This is because they fly slowly enough to allow the Russians enough time to launch their own missiles before the cruise missiles arrive. Yet, as one writer has pointed out, this fact may pose dangers of its own:

> Given the cruise missile's great accuracy and hard-site kill capability, it would be foolish for an adversary either to plan on 'waiting out' a strategic cruise missile attack or to spend large sums of money on silo hardening and defense — thus leaving no recourse but a launch-on-warning strategy. Such a strategy is highly destabilizing because the accidental firing of a cruise missile or misinterpretation of radar data — and the latter is particularly likely given the difficulty of detecting cruise missiles — could trigger a massive retaliatory strike and thus lead to nuclear war.[57]

In short, the case for rejecting the American cruise missiles seems overwhelming.

Nuclear Weapons as a Source of Provocation

The rest of the arguments I shall consider can be stated and discussed relatively briefly. This next argument in particular requires little elaboration. The fundamental idea is that, if Britain were to give up nuclear weapons, and were instead to rely on forms of defence that pose a minimal threat of being used offensively, this would certainly lessen the perceived threat to the Soviet Union. (There is certainly every reason to believe that, rightly or wrongly, the Russians *do* feel threatened by NATO at present.) I mentioned earlier in discussing civil defence why it is best, insofar as it is possible, to avoid presenting a menacing appearance to the Russians: for the more threatened they feel, the more likely they are to act precipitously or impetuously in times of tension. Nuclear weapons breed fear and mistrust, and fear and mistrust tend to push countries closer to war. As Kurt Waldheim, the Secretary-General of the United Nations, has said, 'the arms race is no longer merely an effect of tensions between nations — it has now become one of the causes of such tension'.[58] Thus, insofar as British disarmament would serve to calm Soviet fears concerning the West's intentions, it would to that extent help to minimize a potential source of war.

At the very least, British unilateral disarmament would help to undermine the arguments of the hawks in Russia who claim that NATO is an aggressive alliance and poses a grave threat to Soviet security. By helping to falsify hawkish propaganda within the Soviet Union, British disarmament could serve as a counterpressure against certain forces behind the arms race.

Now, it is certainly true that Britain's existing arsenal is not very provocative. *Polaris*, in particular, is almost exclusively a 'second strike counter-city' weapon. But *Trident* and US cruise missiles are another matter altogether. Both of these are counterforce weapons. The cruise missiles will be liberally spread around close to Russia's borders; they will be capable of striking almost 500 miles deeper into Russian territory than the US F-111s; and they will be wholly under American control. Thus E.P. Thompson's description of the project to install cruise missiles (and *Pershing II*s) as 'nothing less than a slow-playing Cuban missile crisis in reverse' is very apt.[59] (It might be objected here that I have earlier claimed that there are reasons for doubting the effectiveness of cruise missiles; but, if they will not be effective, why should the Russians be so upset about them? There are two replies to this. First, even if the Russians can erect relatively effective defences against cruise missiles, the cost of doing so will be very great. Thus they may regard the development of cruise missiles in Europe as part of an effort to 'break their bank'. Second, even if cruise missiles fail to perform as well as they are intended to, the Russians will still have reason to wonder about our intention in installing them, since our intention was certainly to install weapons that work properly.)

In Chapter I I quoted Lord Hill-Norton as saying that

Trident will have more than double the striking power of *Polaris*. This is rather an understatement. Whereas each *Polaris* submarine carries missiles capable of striking 16 separate targets, each *Trident* submarine will carry missiles capable of striking 128 separate targets. The *Trident* missiles will, moreover, be vastly more accurate. All of this is rather surprising, and may appear somewhat sinister from the Soviet point of view. *Trident* is being billed simply as a replacement for *Polaris*. The arguments for having it require only that it should be capable of destroying 'resources'. It is curious that, while the public is being sold a weapons system for deterring aggression through the threat of retaliation, what it is actually getting is a sophisticated nuclear war-fighting machine. It would be interesting to hear Government proponents of *Trident* explain this.

It should be emphasized that, in arguing against cruise missiles and *Trident* on the ground that they are provocative, I am not advocating appeasement. I have argued in favour of strong defences for Britain. My point here is simply that the defences Britain adopts should be calculated to arouse as little fear and suspicion as possible. In other words, they should be genuinely *defensive*.

The Analogy With Proliferation

A further argument for the abandonment by Britain of some or all nuclear weapons is based on the claim that there is an analogy between keeping nuclear weapons once one already has them and acquiring them if one does not. Insofar as this analogy holds, it is to that extent to be expected that many of the arguments against the spread of nuclear weapons to other countries will also apply to the retention of nuclear weapons by those countries which already possess them. If we disapprove of the spread of nuclear weapons to other countries, then there is a presumption in favour of thinking that we should also disapprove of the continued possession of nuclear weapons by those countries which already have them.

The analogy between retention and acquisition is, however, admittedly imperfect. The acquisition of nuclear weapons by hitherto non-nuclear states may serve to destabilize the existing web of deterrence relations, while the mere retention of nuclear weapons may help to preserve the stability of those relations. Thus retaining nuclear weapons may for this reason be significantly different from acquiring them, and, by the same token, relinquishing them may be different from refraining from acquiring them. In the case of the US and the USSR, between whom the central deterrence relation exists, the analogy may collapse almost entirely.

We need to ask, therefore, whether in Britain's case giving up nuclear weapons would be destabilizing. This is, in so many words, the question I shall be considering in the final chapter. Anticipating that later discussion, I shall simply assert here my conclusion that British nuclear disarmament, if accompanied by the development of alternative defences, would not be destabilizing. I have argued, moreover, that the scheduled 'modernization' programmes (particularly the cruise missiles project) may themselves be destabilizing. So I shall assume here that British nuclear disarmament would not be destabilizing. (It may seem that my argument here assumes its own conclusion. It will soon be evident that nothing actually hinges on this.)

The claim that British disarmament would not be destabilizing requires some qualification. It is possible that the US has in Britain certain strategic support facilities whose removal would be destabilizing. I do not know whether this is the case; I suggest it only as a possibility. It might be, for example, that the Fylingdales Ballistic Missile Early Warning Station is a vital component of the US early warning system, so that, if it were removed, this would make the Americans more fearful of a surprise Soviet first strike and perhaps even make the Russians more confident about their ability to conduct a disabling first strike. (Again, I do not know how important Fylingdales actually is. But let us suppose that it is important for the reason I have given.) Also, Fylingdales is not, so far as I know, in any way provocative. It does not, for example, enhance America's ability to launch a first strike. If these suppositions about Fylingdales were true, then it would be on balance destabilizing if Fylingdales were closed down: for it would make the Russians more trigger-happy, and the Americans more prone to panic. If there are any such American support systems in Britain whose presence is not provocative and whose removal would be destabilizing, then they should probably be allowed to remain — even if they would be targets in a nuclear war. It seems to me that our primary aim must be the prevention of war. The aim of minimizing the damage to Britain in the event of a war is secondary.

If I am right in thinking that British nuclear disarmament would on the whole not be destabilizing, then the analogy between retention and acquisition should here be fairly strong. And in fact many of the reasons for thinking that proliferation is undesirable also count against the retention of nuclear weapons by Britain. Foremost among these is the fact that, when a country undertakes to defend itself by threatening nuclear retaliation against aggressors, it thereby ensures that any external threat to its own security will be automatically transformed into a threat to world survival. This is because any regional conflict involving the use of nuclear weapons has the potential for escalating into a global conflagration. This sort of fear is at present perhaps most acute with regard to Israel, but it is not altogether absent in the case of Britain. Do the people of Britain really wish to rely on a mode of defence which imperils the survival of the rest of mankind — which puts at risk the very existence of future generations?

Another reason for condemning proliferation is that it increases the risk of accidental nuclear war. We have already discussed this problem as it applies to the superpowers, but it is worth pointing out that, other things being equal, the more nuclear weapons there are, the greater the risk of accidental nuclear war is. This is because the more nuclear weapons there are, the greater the probability is that one of them will be fired accidentally or as the result of an error of judgement. It is, therefore, a good reason for Britain to get rid of nuclear weapons that this would decrease the risk of accidental nuclear war.

A third reason for objecting to proliferation is that it increases the likelihood that a nuclear weapon will explode by accident, causing an enormous number of deaths in the area where it goes off. Earlier I claimed that the probability of a nuclear weapon going off by accident is slight, but that does not mean that it cannot happen. In 1961, in Goldsboro, North Carolina, a B-52 bomber carrying two 24-megaton bombs crashed. On one of these bombs, five of the six safety locks had failed. A single switch prevented the bomb from exploding — a bomb which was 1,800 times more powerful than the Hiroshima bomb. Accidents involving nuclear weapons have also occurred in Britain, though the Ministry of Defence has tried to deceive the public about this.[60] On 26 July 1956 a B-47 nuclear bomber crashed directly on top of a nuclear weapons storage site at RAF Lakenheath. Three atomic bombs were badly damaged, and US women and children were evacuated from the base. It is not improbable that something of this sort will eventually happen again, perhaps with far worse consequences.

A fourth reason why proliferation is undesirable is that it increases the probability that nuclear weapons will fall into the hands of terrorists. The presence of nuclear weapons in Britain gives terrorists here easier access to nuclear weapons than they would otherwise have. Although terrorism is not as big a problem in Britain as it is in many other countries, the prospect of nuclear weapons falling into the hands of the IRA is certainly very frightening.

Finally, a fifth reason for objecting to proliferation which may also apply to the retention of nuclear weapons by Britain is that the presence of additional nuclear powers is likely to serve as an impediment to the progress of arms control negotiations. As we have seen, the top table argument attempts to stand this objection on its head by claiming that British participation in arms control negotiations must be beneficial. Probably most countries believe that the participation of their representatives would be beneficial. This view is, however, probably less the product of reason than it is the product of simple national conceit.

There are, of course, other objections to proliferation which do not count against Britain's retaining nuclear weapons. One is that proliferation tends to beget further proliferation. India, for example, was motivated to acquire the bomb at least partly by fears raised by China's having acquired it, and fear of the Indian bomb is largely responsible for Pakistan's efforts to acquire it. But it is highly unlikely that fear of the British bomb will lead anyone else to acquire it, or that this alleged fear could serve as a plausible excuse for anyone's building one. Another cause for alarm about proliferation is the prospect of the irresponsible use of nuclear weapons by a fanatical or messianic national leader. There is relatively little chance of this occurring in Britain.

A further implication of the analogy between retention and acquisition is that arguments designed to justify the retention of nuclear weapons by Britain often implicitly justify proliferation. For example, of the arguments discussed in Chapter II, at least five — the last resort deterrent argument, the nuclear blackmail argument, the prestige 'argument', the positive version of the influence argument, and the top table argument — could be used, *mutatis mutandis*, by countries aspiring to possess nuclear weapons. Indeed, as we have seen, India has already begun to use two of these arguments. If these arguments justify Britain's having nuclear weapons, then they should serve equally well to justify any other country in having them.[61]

The Force of Example Argument

A related line of argument in favour of British nuclear disarmament is intended to show that this might help to inhibit the spread of nuclear weapons to other countries. There are two reasons for thinking that this might be the case. The first is that the retention of nuclear weapons, and in particular the 'modernization' of the British arsenal, may encourage proliferation, so that the refusal to retain or acquire these weapons may at least eliminate this one source of encouragement. As we have seen, other countries may be persuaded by British arguments in favour of retaining nuclear weapons that there are important advantages to be gained by having these weapons — or they may at least appeal to these arguments for justification. At a minimum, they could cite the British example by way of an excuse. It is important to remember that Britain, having ratified the Non-Proliferation

Treaty of 1968 (NPT), is pledged to pursue nuclear disarmament. States aspiring to join the 'nuclear club' might cite the fact that Britain (along with the US and the USSR) has done little or nothing to fulfil its obligations under the NPT as a reason for withholding or withdrawing their own commitment to that treaty. There are already growing signs that, because the three nuclear signatories to the treaty have done so little to honour their obligations, many non-nuclear signatories have begun to regard the treaty as something of a trick designed to perpetuate their positions of inferiority *vis-à-vis* the nuclear powers.

A second and rather stronger claim is that, as well as removing a source of encouragement to proliferation, British nuclear disarmament might actually have a positively inhibiting effect on proliferation. This is not to say that it might actually *reverse* the process — for example, that China or France might be moved to give up the bomb if Britain were to do so. It is only to say that Britain's example, and the reasoning behind it, might help to discourage certain non-nuclear countries from developing their own nuclear arsenals. Britain's gesture would provide dramatic testimony for the view that the risks that go with having nuclear weapons may outweigh the benefits, that the value of these weapons has hitherto been overestimated, and that there are alternative means of defence which may be equally if not more effective. Of course, the effect of Britain's example would almost certainly be indirect; that is, Britain could hope to influence world leaders mainly by influencing world opinion, thereby strengthening the hand of the opponents of nuclear weapons within those countries with a potential for developing nuclear weapons.

These assumptions about the possible effects of British disarmament have been rejected by Lawrence Freedman. He writes that

There is no evidence that unilateral action by Britain, however drastic, will have anything other than a marginal effect on the attitudes and behaviour of non-nuclear weapons states ... Those who argue that to abandon the force would, in its exemplary wisdom, galvanize the

enlightened opinion of mankind into steps to rid the world
of these awful weapons exaggerate the extent to which
countries would allow this to influence their own strategic
calculations. It would be seen more as a symptom of
Britain's decline than an impressive gesture.[62]

It is probably true that the chances are slight that British
disarmament would have a significant impact on the behaviour
of other states, nuclear or non-nuclear. But, where the stakes
are high, even small probabilities can be important. It is a
mistake, moreover, to suggest that disarmament would be
regarded as symptomatic of Britain's decline. It would be
seen in this light only if it were unaccompanied by measures
designed to compensate for the absence of nuclear weapons.
But, if Britain were vigorously to pursue the development of
alternative defences, such as those proposed earlier, then
there would be no grounds for the claim that Britain had
disarmed as a result of economic or political weakness.
(Similar remarks apply to Jonathan Alford's claim that 'the
decision to maintain or discontinue an independent strategic
deterrent will ... be interpreted as a clear indication of
resolve or lack of it'.[63] There are ways of expressing resolve
other than by maintaining a nuclear force.)

The Top Table Overturned

I mentioned earlier that, since additional parties to a negotiation tend to complicate the negotiation and impede its
progress, Britain might accomplish more by resigning its seat
at the top table than by remaining there. This is just the
negative side of a more positive argument which asserts that
Britain could press more earnestly for disarmament, and with
greater effectiveness, if it were to disarm. It is very difficult
for a member of the nuclear club to press for disarmament
from within, for the position of the reformer within the
club is always one of complicity: the reformer's hands are as
dirty as those of the others, and the others know this. Indian
officials are now telling us that the nuclear powers will listen
more attentively to Indian appeals for disarmament once

India gets the bomb. But it is clear that this is false (and that the officials know that it is) and that the nuclear powers will only smile in amusement if India begins to lecture on the evils of the bomb once it has succeeded in its frantic efforts to acquire one. (Countries aspiring to acquire the bomb will also smile.) India will then be implicated in the whole dirty business — will have sanctioned it — and will have forfeited its right to criticize. This is Britain's position now. At present, while the Government is busy disseminating propaganda in support of its policy of acquiring ever more and better nuclear weapons, it is difficult for Britain to press for disarmament without exposing itself to the charge of hypocrisy.

It is significant that the countries which have been most adamant in urging disarmament, and which have taken the lead in sponsoring diplomatic initiatives designed to pave the way for disarmament, have been countries, like Sweden, which neither possess nuclear weapons nor aspire to possess them. It is also significant, and something which those who accept the top table argument must contend with, that Canada has recently decided to remove all nuclear weapons from its soil, with the consequence that it 'seems to have more presence rather than less where disarmament forums convene, and where peace-keeping forces are designed'.[64] It is not unlikely that the same would happen to Britain it if were to follow Canada's lead. As a member of NATO and a trusted ally of the US, and as a country with considerable familiarity with and understanding of the practical obstacles to achieving disarmament, Britain would be in a uniquely favourable position to promote the cause of disarmament if it could approach this task with clean hands.

Moral Arguments

There is a class of arguments against the retention of nuclear weapons by Britain which is of a distinctly moral character. (This is not to deny that there is a sense in which many of the arguments considered earlier are also moral arguments.) There are more arguments in this class than I have space to discuss, and even the ones that I shall consider deserve a far more thorough and detailed examination than I can provide here. Arguments in moral philosophy can become very intricate and highly technical, and it would be inappropriate in a book of this character to become too deeply involved in the complexities of this sort of argument. So, instead of probing deeply into the moral arguments, I shall simply state them and then offer a few brief comments. In the case of the first two arguments, which are the two most common ones, I shall state very briefly why I do not accept them. What I shall say will not be sufficient to refute them, but it seems preferable to treat them in this cursory and unsatisfactory way than to ignore them altogether. What I shall have to say may at least have the merit of helping some people who object to nuclear deterrence to sort out in their own minds whether they object to deterrence on intrinsic moral grounds or whether their objection is simply that deterrence may not work. For readers who wish to explore the moral arguments more carefully, I shall provide references in the footnotes to further reading.

The first argument I shall consider is intended to show that the strategy of nuclear deterrence is immoral. It has as a premiss the claim that the actual use of nuclear weapons would inevitably violate one or both of two of the traditional criteria of 'the just war'. These two criteria are:

(1) *The Criterion of Proportionality*. This states that the level of force employed should be proportional to the aim it is intended to achieve.
(2) *The Criterion of Discrimination*. This states that force should be used in a way which discriminates between combatants and noncombatants.[65]

These seem to be plausible principles, though I myself would not accept them as absolutes. It also seems clear that most uses of nuclear weapons would violate one or both of these criteria. Certainly any direct attacks on Soviet cities would violate the criterion of discrimination. Yet there are certain uses of nuclear weapons which may not violate either criterion. Limited counterforce strikes against Soviet military installations might be discriminate, in that they would not be intended to kill noncombatants, and they could conceivably be proportionate, in that it might genuinely be believed that they could lead to a favourable settlement of the conflict. (Of course, it is difficult to believe that counterforce strikes could have this effect unless they were backed up by the threat to attack cities, and these latter attacks would violate the criterion of discrimination.) Also, certain battlefield nuclear weapons, such as the neutron bomb, might be used in ways which satisfy both criteria. (This is rather surprising, since the neutron bomb has been heavily censured on moral grounds.) If I am right that certain uses of nuclear weapons might not violate the criteria of the just war, then this first moral argument is more limited in scope than is often supposed. At most it shows that *some* uses of nuclear weapons would be immoral.

Simply to show that certain uses of nuclear weapons would be immoral is not, however, to show that the possession of nuclear weapons for purposes of deterrence is immoral, even if the weapons could not be used without violating the just war criteria. A further premiss is needed in order to generate the conclusion that it is immoral to possess nuclear weapons for purposes of deterrence. There are two principles which are usually appealed to in the course of this argument. These are:

(a) It is wrong to threaten to do that which it would be wrong to do.
(b) It is wrong to intend, even conditionally, to do that which it would be wrong to do.[66]

The first of these seems to me totally implausible. I shall not discuss it here, for it is not clear to me how it could be either attacked or defended. The second principle seems more plausible, and has in fact been held by a number of traditional moralists. (There is a traditional moral principle which states that 'morality inheres in the intention as well as in the action'.)

The reason that I am unable to accept this second principle stems from my allegiance to one of two rival conceptions of the nature of morality. According to the view which I accept, what matters for morality is primarily what *happens* as a result of what moral agents do. Because it holds that morality is primarily concerned with consequences, this conception of morality is called 'consequentialism'. According to the rival view, the focus of morality is primarily on the *agent himself* — his dispositions, intentions, integrity, and the intrinsic character of what he does. If one holds this non-consequentialist view, then one may think that it matters greatly if a person intends to act in a way that is wrong — even if he will never in fact act in that way. Indeed, one may believe that his having this intention is every bit as wrong as his actually acting on it would be. If, on the other hand, one is a consequentialist, one will think that it matters much less if a person has an evil intention as long as he never in fact acts on it. Indeed, if the person's merely having this intention succeeds in preventing certain very undesirable events from occurring (as may be true in certain cases in which nuclear deterrence holds), then the consequentialist will welcome the fact that the person has this intention.

Now, it is not in itself an objection to the principle about intentions that it presupposes a non-consequentialist conception of morality. In order for this to be an objection, it would need to be shown that consequentialism is the correct conception of the nature of morality, and this is obviously too large a task to be undertaken here. But I have thought it worthwhile simply to point out that the principle does conflict with this one widely held conception of the nature of morality. This will at least explain why many of us cannot accept it.

The second argument I shall mention is the pacifist argument. There are a great many different doctrines of pacifism. I shall not try to distinguish the various versions, but shall simply consider what seems to me the most common as well as the most morally forceful understanding of the doctrine. Thus, by 'pacifism' I shall mean the doctrine which holds that, whatever the consequences, one ought never to use violence, or to threaten to use violence, even implicitly through the possession of the means of violence. This doctrine clearly prohibits the policy of nuclear deterrence. It also condemns the various types of non-nuclear defence which involve the potential use of violence — that is, it objects to conventional defences and to territorial defence.

Like the first argument we considered, pacifism pre-supposes a non-consequentialist conception of morality. According to consequentialism, what matters is the prevention or minimization of violence. This means that, if one can prevent a greater amount of violence only by acting violently oneself, then, other things being equal, one ought to act violently.[67] Whereas the consequentialist's concern is focused on the *victims* of violence, the pacifist's concern is focused primarily on the *agent*. The pacifist believes that what matters most is that one ought not *oneself* to act violently, even if this means that more violence will be done.

Pacifism seems to attribute too much importance to the avoidance of dirty hands. As Jonathan Glover has said, with regard to a principle which is similar to pacifism in this respect,

> [it] tells us to keep our hands clean, at a cost which will probably be paid by other people. It is excessively self-regarding, placing considerations either of my own feelings or purity of character far too high on the scale of factors to be considered.[68]

Glover has also criticized pacifism on the ground that it depends on the view that there is an intrinsic moral difference between deliberately acting to bring about a certain outcome and allowing the outcome to come about by deliberately omitting to prevent it. If this view is false, and I myself believe that it is,[69] then the pacifist cannot preserve his moral purity simply by refusing to act violently himself. For his purity will be violated if he allows violence to occur which he could have prevented by the exercise of a lesser amount of violence.[70]

Again, these remarks are not by themselves fatal to paci-fism. But, by exposing some of the underlying assumptions of the pacifist view, they may at least help some people who are attracted to pacifism to decide whether it is consistent with other moral views they hold.[71]

Thus far I have noted that my opposition to the two most

common moral arguments stems from the fact that they are non-consequentialist in character. The question now arises whether there is a moral argument against nuclear deterrence which is consequentialist in character. The answer is that there is such an argument.[72] Stated simply, it is as follows. The consequentialist holds that most uses of nuclear weapons, and perhaps all uses against centres of population, would be wrong. This is because he believes that any benefits which might be gained through the use of nuclear weapons would be almost certainly outweighed by the vast amount of harm which the use of these weapons would cause. He concedes, however, that it is permissible, or perhaps in some cases morally required, to threaten to use nuclear weapons if the threat will succeed in preventing undesirable events from occurring.[73] Yet the problem with this is that there is no guarantee that the threat will succeed. And, in the case of nuclear deterrence, if the threat does not succeed, our leaders may carry out their threat, and in doing so they would be acting in a way that would be seriously morally wrong.

In each particular case, therefore, the consequentialist holds that we must consider both the risks and the possible benefits of following nuclear deterrence, and compare them with the risks and possible benefits of pursuing an alternative policy. Among the relevant questions here are: How likely is it that nuclear deterrence would fail? What would the probable consequences be for the people living in the country of our adversary if nuclear deterrence were to fail? What would the probable consequences be for us if nuclear deterrence were to fail? What would the probable consequences be both for us and for the people in the country of our adversary if we were to abandon nuclear deterrence and instead follow an alternative policy? If the policy of nuclear deterrence compares unfavourably with an alternative policy in terms of the risks they each involve and the benefits they each offer (taking probabilities into account), then the consequentialist will hold that it would be immoral to follow the policy of nuclear deterrence.

Whether or not this argument implies that Britain ought to abandon nuclear deterrence will depend on the answers to the various questions I have just cited. Whether or not the consequentialist argument applies depends on what the facts are. Thus it may apply in the case of one country but not in the case of another, since the circumstances of the two countries may be very different. It is, in other words, not an absolutist argument.

Clearly, however, if we decide that, all things considered, the consequences for Britain and its allies of Britain's abandoning nuclear weapons would probably be better than the consequences of its retaining them, then it will almost certainly follow that the consequentialist argument would apply in the case of Britain. For the moment I shall leave the consequentialist argument open-ended, since the question whether it would be better for Britain and its allies if Britain were to abandon nuclear weapons is the subject of the concluding chapter.

Better 'Red' or Dead?

The question whether it would be better for Britain to fall under Soviet rule or to suffer nuclear annihilation has entered the discussion at several points in this book. While I think that we can answer the question whether or not Britain should have nuclear weapons quite independently of the question whether it would be better to be 'red' or dead, the latter question nevertheless often turns up in discussions about British disarmament, and it would be a mistake to ignore it here. I shall argue that those who claim that nuclear destruction would be better than Soviet rule are wrong. Several of the points I shall mention in support of this contention were stated earlier by Bertrand Russell. At a time when the American National Security Advisor can be heard to proclaim that 'better red than dead' is a 'contemptible slogan',[74] they are worth repeating.

The question whether one would prefer to be red or dead oneself is presumably equivalent to the question whether one would find life worth living under Soviet rule. Here I think it is certainly relevant to note that most people who actually live under Soviet rule do find life worth living. I do not have any statistics at my fingertips, but I would be very surprised if the suicide rates in Soviet-dominated countries were much higher, if at all, than those in Western countries. Of course, the fact that people in Soviet-dominated countries on the whole find their lives worth living does not entail that, if we had lives like theirs, we would find them worth living. While they might find a life without certain freedoms worth living, we might not. Their preferences may simply be different from ours. It might even be held that their preferences have been distorted through manipulation. Or it might be that they simply are not vividly aware of all that is lacking in their lives, and that, if they were, their preferences might be different. On the other hand, while they may be largely unaware of what life in free countries is like, it is equally true that they have a much better idea of what life in a Soviet-dominated country is like than we do. Most of us are quite ignorant of what life is really like for most people in Soviet-dominated countries, and therefore we should not be too hasty to judge that we would not find that sort of life worth living. Perhaps if we were to have sufficient experience of life under Soviet rule, we would come to prefer it to death just as most people do who actually have that sort of life.

Some people may agree that they might eventually come to prefer life under communism to death, but, from their present perspective, they would regard this possible future attitude as the result of an erosion or corruption of their present values. They might think that it really would be better for them to be dead rather than red, even though, if they were red, they would prefer to go on living. And, if they think that their hypothetical future preference for being red rather than dead would simply be a mistake, then they may also take this view of the actual preferences of people now living under Soviet rule. That is, they may believe that it would in fact be better for people in Soviet-dominated countries if they were dead. That the people in these countries do not themselves believe this shows only that they are mistaken. If a proponent of nuclear weapons could honestly persuade himself to take this view, it might help to soothe his conscience over the thought that our leaders may one day put those people in Soviet-dominated countries out of their alleged misery.

Suppose that you would prefer to be dead rather than live under Soviet rule. If you have thought carefully about the matter, and have looked closely at what ordinary life in Soviet-dominated countries is like, and if you have taken into account what your view might be if you had actually lived under Soviet rule for a while, then I would not quarrel with your judgement. But remember that this is a judgement about what you would prefer for yourself. It is not equivalent to the judgement that it would be better for Britain to suffer massive nuclear bombardment than to fall under Soviet rule. To prefer nuclear destruction to Soviet domination is not simply to prefer individual death to life under Soviet rule; it is to prefer near-universal death to Soviet rule.

Those who, in the name of freedom, would actually prefer to see Britain destroyed by nuclear weapons than to see it ruled by the Russians are guilty of inconsistency. Supposedly in defence of freedom, they would deny us the most fundamental freedom: the freedom to determine our fate, to decide for ourselves whether to live or die.[75] On the other hand, it is a consistent position to prefer death for oneself to life under Soviet rule and at the same time to prefer to see Britain ruled by the Russians than destroyed by nuclear weapons. This position respects people's freedom to choose. If Britain were to be conquered by the Russians, then those who would prefer death could either commit suicide or face death in resisting Soviet rule. There is no reason why they should insist on everyone else dying with them. Those who would prefer capitulation to death could also have their preference. In other words, there is an asymmetry between the options of nuclear destruction and Soviet domination: while Soviet domination would allow those who would prefer death to have their preference, nuclear destruction would not allow those who would prefer continued existence to have their preference.

(It might be objected that many of those who would prefer death to life under Soviet rule might be prevented from commiting suicide by the belief that suicide is immoral. But it is difficult to see how one could regard suicide as immoral and at the same time regard it as permissible to drop nuclear bombs on Russian cities. More importantly, if someone would prefer death but finds suicide immoral, then that is, to put it callously, his own hard luck. He has no right to demand that we should all die in order to enable him to escape from an unpleasant existence without having to sacrifice his own moral purity.)

Suppose that most or even all of us would find life under Soviet rule to be worse than death. Would it then be reasonable to prefer nuclear annihilation to Soviet conquest? I am myself inclined to doubt that it would; for it is not only our own welfare that is at stake. Nuclear warfare puts at peril the lives of people the world over. It endangers not only the welfare but even the very existence of future generations. There is a very strong case for thinking that, even if Russian domination would be *for us* worse than death, it would nevertheless be better if we were to endure it rather than risk the destruction of so much life in other countries.

Suppose that the outcome of the Cuban missile crisis had been different, and the US and the Soviet Union had gone to war. This would have caused many millions of deaths in countries totally uninvolved in the conflict, and might even have brought life on earth to an end. (It is doubtful that it would have ended life on earth, but no one really knows what the consequences of a large-scale nuclear war would be. Many of the consequences of nuclear war have been discovered only by accident, and there are surely other potential consequences which remain unknown.) If the superpowers had actually gone to war, would this not have been a monstrous crime against humanity, totally unjustifiable in terms of whatever it was they were seeking to defend? Even now, are the ideological squabbles between the two superpowers really sufficiently important to justify their putting at risk the lives of every man, woman, and child on this planet? If not, then we should think along similar lines about a potential nuclear conflict in Western Europe. Even if we ourselves would prefer the nuclear destruction of Britain and Western Europe to domination by the Soviet Union, would we have the right to act on that preference if it would involve the deaths of many millions of people outside of Europe?

A final point which should be mentioned in this connection is that, while the nuclear destruction of Britain might bring a permanent end to free human life on these islands, it is impossible to believe that a Soviet tyranny here could last forever. As Bertrand Russell once said,

> A victory of Communism might be as disastrous as the barbarian destruction of the Roman Empire, but there is no reason to think that it would be more disastrous than that event. While the human race survives, humaneness, love of liberty, and a civilized way of life will, sooner or later, prove irresistably attractive. The progress of mankind has always been a matter of ups and downs. The downs have always seemed final to contemporaries ... Any person who supposes that the evils of Communism, if it achieved a supremacy, would last forever is allowing himself to be so limited by the heat of present controversies as to be unable to see their similarity to equally virulent controversies in the past or to realize that a dark age, if it is upon us, like the dark ages in the past will not last forever.[76]

IV
SUMMARY AND CONCLUSION

In this concluding chapter I shall summarize the results of the various arguments for and against the weapons systems in each of the three categories mentioned earlier — namely, American forward-based systems, NATO TNW, and independent strategic nuclear weapons. After seeing how the pros and cons add up with regard to the weapons in each category, I shall take what I think is the strongest proposal for a defence policy which calls for the retention of nuclear weapons and compare it with a general proposal for an alternative, non-nuclear defence policy. The comparison will be conducted in terms of the four criteria stated earlier on pages 69-70.

American Forward-Based Systems

There are basically four arguments which favour allowing American forward bases and forward-based weapons to remain in Britain. I shall restate them here very briefly.

(a) *The first version of the trigger argument* holds that American forward-based systems serve to 'couple' European and American security by posing an implicit threat that any war in Europe will escalate to the strategic level.
(b) *The negative version of the influence argument* holds that Britain will forfeit its influence over American policy if it demands the removal of American bases.
(c) *The multilateralist's argument* holds that American forward-based systems should not be removed without

gaining matching concessions from the Russians.

(d) *The contribution to NATO argument* holds that, since Britain derives benefits from its alliance with the US, it owes it to the US to allow these bases to remain.

Of these four arguments, the first three have been heavily criticized. Taken together, these first three arguments would add up to a very flimsy case for allowing the American bases to remain. The fourth argument, however, seems stronger. If having these bases in Britain strengthens NATO's deterrent, from which Britain benefits, then Britain ought to allow them to remain. The matter is not, however, quite so simple. It is not the case that *all* of the American facilities serve to strengthen deterrence. Not all American military deployments are guaranteed to serve the interests of deterrence. In the case of many of the American facilities and weapons systems, there seems to be a noticeable lack of any strong military justification for their being here. I have not, for example, been able to discover any very impressive reasons for having F-111 nuclear bombers in Britain. But if they do not make an important contribution to NATO's deterrent, then Britain will not be under a strong obligation to the US to allow them to be stationed here.

On the other hand, it must be allowed that there may be some facilities which do make an important contribution to the defence of Europe or to the maintenance of a stable relation of mutual deterrence between the superpowers. If so, then this provides a strong reason for allowing these facilities to remain. It is, of course, not possible here to go down the list of US facilities in Britain and decide to which ones the contribution to NATO argument most applies. But one deserves particular mention. If we decide that the problem of nuclear blackmail is sufficiently serious to make us welcome the presence of the American nuclear umbrella, then it will be difficult for us to demand that the US submarine base at Holy Loch be closed down. For in this case we would be seeking to benefit from the American strategic deterrent, but at the same time we would be damaging its effectiveness by refusing to share the risks of having it. (The closure of the port would mean that fewer American submarines could be at sea at a given time.) So the contribution to NATO argument seems to provide a strong reason for retaining at least *some* of the American facilities in Britain.

Against this, there are five arguments which favour the removal of American forward bases and forward-based weapons. These are as follows.

(a) *The prudential argument* holds that American forward-based systems and strategic support facilities ought to be removed on the ground that they provide targets for nuclear strikes in any war in which the US and the Soviet Union are involved. It also holds that American forward-based nuclear weapons are dangerous in that they help to enable the US to fight a nuclear war with the Soviet Union that is 'limited' to the European theatre.

(b) The argument that *nuclear weapons are provocative* holds that it would decrease international tensions if American nuclear weapons were removed from areas so near to the Soviet Union's borders.

(c) *The analogy with proliferation* suggests that the stationing of American nuclear weapons in Britain increases the risk of a nuclear accident and of nuclear terrorism.

(d) *The force of example argument* holds that Britain will be seen as continuing implicitly to affirm the value of nuclear weapons, thereby indirectly encouraging proliferation, if it allows American nuclear weapons to remain.

(e) *The clean hands argument* (see the section entitled 'The Top Table Overturned') asserts that Britain will be less able to press effectively for disarmament as long as it allows nuclear weapons to be stationed on its soil.

The first of these arguments provides a powerful reason for removing all of the US bases and nuclear weapons systems which would be targets for preemptive strikes by the Soviet Union. Britain is a small and densely populated country, and the risks which it is being asked to accept in having the country extensively covered with American military bases are excessive. Also, having American nuclear weapons in Britain is destabilizing, since it helps to encourage the belief that the

US could fight a 'limited' nuclear war in Europe. The second of these five arguments also has a certain amount of force. Having once risked nuclear war to prevent the Russians from installing nuclear missiles near its borders, the US should recognize that the removal of certain nuclear weapons stationed near Russia's borders would help to ease East-West tensions. The remaining three arguments seem less powerful, though each clearly has some force.

The conclusion that I would draw from this comparison of the arguments for and against American forward bases and forward-based weapons systems is that, while the arguments clearly favour the removal of US nuclear weapons and many if not most of the US facilities, the arguments are neverthe-less more finely balanced with regard to a few of the strategic support facilities — in particular, the submarine base at Holy Loch. What we decide about this particular facility will depend on what our considered view of the problem of nuclear blackmail is. I shall return to this problem shortly.

NATO Theatre and Tactical Nuclear Weapons

The weapons in this category include the British-manned bombers carrying nuclear bombs under single-key British control, the battlefield nuclear weapons under double-key control which are operated by the BAOR, and the proposed cruise missiles. The arguments which support the possession of these weapons are as follows.

(a) *The first version of the trigger argument* holds that TNW under the double-key system serve to couple European and American security.
(b) *The second version of the trigger argument* holds that TNW under single-key British control could be used to trigger the release of TNW under double-key control, and that this reinforces deterrence in Europe.
(c) *The free-rider argument* holds that Britain would be unfairly seeking a free-ride within NATO in refusing to operate TNW or have them stationed on its soil.
(d) *The negative version of the influence argument* holds

that Britain will weaken its influence over American policy
if it refuses to have TNW.

(e) *The contribution to NATO argument* holds that on
balance Britain benefits from the fact that NATO employs
TNW, and so Britain ought to share the risks involved in
having them.

I have earlier suggested why I think that the first two of
these arguments, which are the two main strategic rationales
for having TNW, are unimpressive. And, if the military reasons
for having TNW are unimpressive, then it is unlikely that the
contribution to NATO argument will provide a strong reason
for having them. Indeed, the contribution to NATO argument is not even compatible with the second version of the
trigger argument. The free-rider argument fails to apply in
this case as long as Britain seeks to replace TNW with alternative, non-nuclear defences. Finally, the negative version of
the influence argument has been shown to be relatively weak.
All things considered, these five arguments fail to provide a
strong case in favour of TNW.

The case against TNW seems far stronger. There are six
arguments for abandoning nuclear weapons which apply to
TNW.

(a) It is argued that *non-nuclear defences* are better for use
on the battlefield than TNW, and constitute a more
credible defensive deterrent.

(b) *The prudential argument* holds that TNW constitute
targets for preemptive nuclear strikes, and also help to
make it possible for the superpowers to fight a 'limited'
nuclear war in Europe.

(c) The argument that *nuclear weapons are provocative*
holds that the installation of cruise missiles will exacerbate
East-West tensions.

(d) *The analogy with proliferation* suggests that TNW, and
especially cruise missiles, increase the likelihood of accidental nuclear war through the accidental or unauthorized
firing of a nuclear weapon. They also increase the probability of an accidental nuclear explosion and of nuclear
terrorism.

(e) *The force of example argument* holds that Britain will be seen as continuing implicitly to affirm the value of nuclear weapons, thereby indirectly encouraging proliferation, if it continues to rely on TNW.

(f) *The clean hands argument* asserts that Britain will be less effective in urging disarmament if it continues to rely on TNW.

The first of these arguments seems very compelling. Most of the six or seven thousand NATO TNW in Europe have ranges of less than 160 kilometers and so would be likely to explode over NATO territory if used in the course of a defensive war.[1] This would cause an incalculable amount of damage within Western Europe. It would also constitute an invitation to the Warsaw Pact to use their nuclear weapons on NATO territory. Thus to use TNW on West European territory in order to try to stop a Russian invasion would be, in the words of Robert Neild, 'an act of self-immolation without precedent'.[2] This fact, combined with the principle that military options which would cause at least as much harm to oneself as to one's enemy are unlikely to deter, yields the conclusion that TNW have very little value as a defensive deterrent. Conventional weapons, such as PGM, would be a more rational investment. This being the case, the contribution to NATO argument has little or no force as it applies to TNW.

The prudential argument is also persuasive in the case of TNW. As we have seen, cruise missiles would be prime targets for a preemptive attack. And they might also be used to strike targets in the non-Soviet parts of Eastern Europe in the course of a 'limited' nuclear war. Both the argument that nuclear weapons are provocative and the analogy with proliferation are quite strong in the case of TNW. If a tactical nuclear weapon deployed at the East-West German border were to explode by accident, this could set the Russian tanks rolling into Western Europe. Finally, the clean hands argument is probably the weakest of the six, but even it is not without force.

The comparison between these two sets of arguments leads me to conclude that the case against TNW is overwhelming.

Independent Strategic Nuclear Weapons

Weighing up the pros and cons with regard to Britain's independent nuclear deterrent is an extremely difficult exercise. This is not only because there are so many arguments on both sides, but also because there are powerful arguments on both sides, and the range of considerations which are relevant in balancing them against each other is large and very complex. Again, I shall begin by briefly restating the arguments which are intended to support the possession of an independent strategic force.

(a) *The second centre* and *last resort deterrent arguments* both claim that the British independent force enhances deterrence in Europe by providing insurance against the failure of the American nuclear guarantee.

(b) *The second version of the trigger argument* holds that the British independent force enhances deterrence in Europe by reinforcing the American nuclear guarantee.

(c) *The free-rider argument* holds that, in giving up its independent force, Britain would be unfairly placing the whole of the burden of maintaining the Alliance's deterrent — from which Britain benefits — on the Americans.

(d) *The nuclear blackmail argument* holds that the independent force provides the most reliable deterrent against nuclear blackmail during a European war.

(e) *The positive and negative versions of the influence argument* both hold that, without its own strategic force, Britain would lose much of its influence over American policy-making.

(f) *The top table argument* holds that Britain can best work for disarmament by attending negotiations to which it will be invited only if it has an independent nuclear force.

(g) *The multilateralist's argument* holds that Britain's independent force ought not to be given up except in exchange for matching Soviet concessions.

(h) *The problem of Germany* requires that Britain should not give up its independent force if this would lead Germany to acquire nuclear weapons.

(i) *The contribution to NATO argument* holds that NATO's deterrent would be weakened by British disarmament, so Britain owes it to the other members of the Alliance to retain its independent force.

Many of these arguments I have criticized rather heavily. For example, I would attribute almost no weight at all to the top table argument, or to the multilateralist's argument, nor to either version of the influence argument. Moreover, the free-rider argument is clearly wrong if Britain adopts alternative defences. And if we decide that Britain should rely on the US arsenal for the deterrence of nuclear blackmail, it will be because this is implied by a rational distribution of burdens within the Alliance. The problem of Germany would be a serious problem if the evidence suggested that Germany attaches considerable value to the British force, but in fact the evidence does not suggest this. The second centre argument seems relatively weak, since the independent force is of doubtful value in deterring an invasion of Europe. The last resort deterrent argument, however, seems somewhat stronger. While the independent force has little credibility as a deterrent against limited counterforce strikes, it does have some credibility as a deterrent against an invasion of British territory. And it is highly credible as a deterrent against an all-out nuclear attack on Britain (though the threat of an all-out attack is extremely remote). The trigger argument also has some slight plausibility, though I claimed that, since the possibility of deception has drawbacks as well as advantages, the trigger argument cuts both ways. It is, moreover, incompatible with the free-rider and contribution to NATO arguments.

By far the most powerful argument for the independent deterrent is the nuclear blackmail argument. The threat of retaliation seems to be the most effective deterrent against nuclear blackmail in the event of an invasion of Britain, and is certainly the most effective and possibly the only realistic deterrent against nuclear blackmail in the event of an invasion of Western Europe. The problem of nuclear blackmail is, moreover, an extremely serious problem for those who advocate a strong British conventional commitment to the defence of Europe. For, if Britain were without any way of deterring nuclear blackmail, then the use of nuclear blackmail against Britain could undermine the effectiveness of the British conventional forces in Europe. And, if the Russians feel confident that they could easily win a war in Europe by resorting to nuclear blackmail, this may weaken their inhibitions against invading. In short, if the British have no adequate deterrent against nuclear blackmail, this may make war in Europe more likely. This is why the nuclear blackmail argument is so forceful.

Finally, the contribution to NATO argument is either very weak (since, when viewed simply as an integral component of the NATO arsenal, Britain's force is insignificant), or else it simply repeats the nuclear blackmail argument (since the most important contribution the British force makes to the NATO deterrent is in its role as a deterrent against nuclear blackmail). Either way, we can afford to ignore the contribution to NATO argument as it applies to the independent force.

Next, the arguments which militate against the continued possession of an independent deterrent are as follows.

(a) It is argued that a *non-nuclear defence policy* would be more rational for Britain than the continued reliance on retaliatory deterrence.

(b) *The economic argument* holds that the maintenance of an independent deterrent not only prevents increased spending on conventional and other defences, but is actually necessitating potentially dangerous reductions in Britain's conventional forces.

(c) *The prudential argument* holds that all of the support facilities for the submarine force including the port at Holy Loch would be targets for nuclear strikes in the event of a war involving the US and the Soviet Union.

(d) It is argued that *the dangers of relying on retaliatory deterrence* may outweigh the benefits.

(e) The argument that *nuclear weapons are provocative* holds that *Trident*, as a counterforce weapons system, will serve to aggravate Soviet suspicions as to the West's intentions.

(f) *The analogy with proliferation* suggests that Britain's reliance on retaliatory deterrence poses a threat to world security. It suggests that the abandonment of the independent deterrent would decrease the risk of a nuclear accident and of nuclear terrorism in Britain. It also suggests that Britain's presence at negotiations may impede their progress. Finally, it points out that many arguments in favour of Britain's having an independent deterrent (including the nuclear blackmail argument) implicitly sanction proliferation.

(g) *The force of example argument* holds that Britain's abandonment of the independent deterrent could help to inhibit the spread of nuclear weapons to other countries.

(h) *The clean hands argument* holds that Britain would be better able to press for disarmament if it were to cease to rely on the independent deterrent for its own security.

The first of these arguments is quite general. Whether or not it is correct depends in part on how the other arguments for abandoning the independent deterrent compare with the arguments for retaining it. Since this first argument is clearly the most crucial argument in the book, as well as the most difficult, I shall examine it extensively later in this section.

The economic argument poses a serious problem for the defender of the independent deterrent, but it is open to the defender of the deterrent to reply that, without the independent force, Britain will be unable to deter the use of nuclear blackmail; and then nuclear blackmail might be used to undermine Britain's conventional forces. The economic argument, then, leads back to the dilemma discussed previously in the section on nuclear blackmail, and to which I suggested that a solution might be to rely on the US for the deterrence of nuclear blackmail.

The prudential argument is at its weakest in the case of the independent deterrent, since the submarine force provides relatively few nuclear targets near populated areas — though the base at Holy Loch certainly constitutes a major risk for the inhabitants of Glasgow. If, however, we think that the problem of nuclear blackmail is so serious that Britain must either have an independent force to deter it or must rely on the US deterrent, then it would seem that Britain must accept the risks of having certain nuclear targets on its soil.

I shall not discuss the remaining arguments in detail, though it seems to me that they all have a certain amount of force — especially the implications of the analogy with proliferation and the argument which emphasizes the dangers of retaliatory deterrence. Instead I shall now return to the problem of nuclear blackmail, since the weighing up of the arguments for and against the independent deterrent seems to turn on how strong the nuclear blackmail argument actually is. Most of the case in favour of the independent force rests on the nuclear blackmail argument, and there appears to be no comparably strong argument on the other side. Yet there is a greater number of valid arguments on the other side and, while each alone seems less powerful than the nuclear blackmail argument, together they may add up to a powerful case for abandoning the force. But before we can adequately compare this case with the case for retaining the force, we need to arrive at a better understanding of just how strong the nuclear blackmail argument is.

I have already suggested why I think the nuclear blackmail argument is so powerful. I shall now summarize the various points which can be made in reply to this argument. The first of these points is simply that the threat of nuclear blackmail is extremely remote, since the likelihood of a Soviet invasion is itself very small. Even Lord Chalfont, a leading exponent of the 'Soviet threat theory', concedes that he is 'not kept awake at night by the spectre of the Red hordes sweeping down to the Channel ports; the nightmare is of a more subtle kind'.[3] (He then goes on to discuss 'the cancer within'.) I have, however, admitted that my assessment of the Soviet threat cannot be extended to cover the indefinite future, and I have argued that Britain needs defences adequate to insure against future uncertainties. Nuclear blackmail is one such future possibility.

Second, even if there were a Soviet invasion, the Russian leaders would have several reasons for avoiding nuclear blackmail. They would clearly wish to avoid incurring the domestic and international hostility which the use of nuclear weapons against cities during an aggressive campaign would undoubtedly provoke. Earlier I discounted this particular inhibition against the use of nuclear blackmail in times of war, but it cannot be ignored altogether. Also, the use of nuclear weapons against cities would undermine certain of the political aims underlying the invasion by destroying industrial and other economic resources in the country under attack.

Third, I have argued that there are fearful risks involved in relying on the threat of retaliation in order to deter certain forms of aggression. Even if these risks are more than compensated for in the particular case of nuclear blackmail, there remains the problem that, as long as Britain possesses the means to destroy Soviet cities, it is always possible that these means will be used in a situation in which it would be irrational to do so. By providing our leaders with the most effective means of deterring nuclear blackmail, we thereby expose ourselves to the possibility that our leaders will, through miscalculation or irrationality, act in a way that will result in the destruction of Britain.

Because of the risks involved in retaliatory deterrence, it would be preferable if other ways of deterring nuclear blackmail could be found. I have explained why I think that a system of defence in depth could help to deter the use of nuclear blackmail in the course of an invasion of Britain, but this of course would have no deterrent effect against the use of nuclear blackmail in order to compel the surrender of British troops in Central Europe. So far the only alternative deterrent against this use of nuclear blackmail which I have mentioned is civil defence, and it must be admitted that this alone would not be a very powerful deterrent. Perhaps there are other alternatives — for example, dispersing British forces in Germany in a way that would make a surrender harder to obtain, just as it would be harder to obtain the surrender of a territorial army. (The German strategist Afheldt has put forward a proposal for the defence of West Germany which involves the dispersal of autonomous commando units equipped with precision-guided anti-tank weapons throughout West German territory. A system of defence of this sort might help to deter nuclear blackmail in the same way that having a territorial army might. If, moreover, these units were to attack by stealth, it might be difficult for the Russians to identify the attackers as British.[4]) But I cannot explore these possibilities here.

Finally, as I argued earlier, it is possible to question whether even a British independent force would be adequate to deter the use of nuclear blackmail. To act as a fully credible deterrent, the force would need to be large enough so that at least two and preferably three submarines could be at sea at any given time. But this seems to be beyond Britain's present and foreseeable future financial resources. Moreover, a small submarine force could be rendered obsolete as the result of major advances in ASW or ABM technology. So the problem of nuclear blackmail will remain a serious problem even if Britain eventually deploys the four *Trident* submarines it is scheduled to have. This reflection led me earlier to the proposal that Britain should abandon the attempt to deter nuclear blackmail itself and instead rely on the American strategic arsenal for this purpose. This proposal is reinforced by the claim that it would constitute a rational allocation of burdens within the Alliance.

The main objection to this proposal is that an American threat to retaliate in response to the destruction of a British city is less credible than a British threat would be. There are, however, reasons for thinking that the American threat would be sufficiently credible to serve the purpose of deterrence. First, as I mentioned, it might be possible to integrate British and American forces on the battlefield in such a way that it would be difficult to blackmail the British without indirectly blackmailing the Americans. And in any case if nuclear blackmail were to succeed in compelling the British (and presumably the Germans and others) to surrender, it is difficult to see how the Americans could keep up the fight by themselves; so the American forces would presumably have to surrender as well. But this would be so humiliating that the US might be willing to accept the risks involved in retaliating in order to avoid it. Second, if the US had pledged in advance to defend Britain against nuclear blackmail, then it could avoid retaliating only at the cost of severely damaging the credibility of its deterrent in other situations later in the war which it might regard as more important. Finally, it is clearly plausible that the US would, if nothing else, at least retaliate against cities in Eastern (non-Soviet) Europe. This would carry with it a minimal risk of retaliation against American cities. But it would be apparent to the Russians from the start that they and the US leaders could continue on a tit-for-tat basis to destroy the cities of each other's allies until there were no more cities left in Europe. And they would realize that this would be an utterly fruitless exercise to become involved in (as well as one which would dump more fallout on them than on the Americans), and so they would be disinclined to make the first strike in the series.

The West Germans have to rely on the US for the deterrence of nuclear blackmail, and this evidently does not cause them to despair over the prospect of their conventional forces being undermined by blackmail in the event of an invasion. (I mentioned earlier that the nuclear blackmail argument implicitly sanctions proliferation. If the American guarantee were not credible, then the nuclear blackmail argument would provide Germany with a strong reason for acquiring an independent strategic nuclear force. This suggests that it might in fact help to discourage the Germans from ever building their own bombs if Britain were to reaffirm its faith in the American nuclear guarantee by openly relying on this guarantee for the deterrence of nuclear blackmail.)

This proposal will clearly not seem satisfactory to everyone. Some people will think that the threat of nuclear blackmail is so serious that nothing short of a British independent deterrent can be trusted to deal with it. And others will be unhappy with any proposal that does not permit Britain to cease altogether to rely on nuclear weapons — its own or anyone else's. But if the problem of nuclear blackmail is as potentially serious as I have suggested it might be, then it may not be possible for Britain reasonably to avoid relying on nuclear weapons at some point.

Having examined the nuclear blackmail argument in some detail, we are now in a position to weigh up the arguments for and against the independent deterrent and arrive at a judgement. Clearly the arguments are much more finely balanced here than in the case of American forward-based systems or NATO TNW. This being the case, it seems to me that the most illuminating way of judging the case for independent nuclear weapons will be to compare a defence policy based on the possession of an independent deterrent with a wholly non-nuclear defence policy based on the types of alternative defence I mentioned earlier. I shall exclude American forward-based systems and TNW from the comparison, since, because their disadvantages outweigh their advantages, to include them would be to prejudice the comparison in favour of the non-nuclear policy.

As the standards for the comparison I shall, as promised, use the four criteria set forth early in the last chapter. These are:

(1) Under which of the two policies would the risk of nuclear war in Europe be less?
(2) Under which policy would the risk of conventional war in Europe be less?
(3) Under which policy would the risk of Britain's being dominated or occupied by a foreign power be less?
(4) Under which policy would the expected damage resulting from a war in Europe be less?

Now, it is unlikely that either policy will be able to satisfy all four of these criteria. It is more likely that some of the criteria will be satisfied by one policy and some by the other. If this is the case, then which policy will be deemed superior will depend on two things. First, it will depend on how important one thinks certain criteria are in comparison with certain others. And, second, it will depend upon the *extent* to which the various criteria are satisfied. (For example, one policy might make nuclear war only slightly less likely than it would be under the other, while making the amount of damage that would probably result if war were to occur far greater than it would be under the other.)

Different people are likely to gauge the importance of the various criteria differently. Thus the disagreement over whether it would be better to be 'red' or dead would emerge as a disagreement over the relative importance of criteria (1) and (3). On the other hand, we can expect a considerable amount of agreement as to the way in which certain criteria should be ranked. Most of us, for example, would find criterion (1) to be more important than criterion (2) — that is, we would attribute more importance to reducing the risk of nuclear war than to reducing the risk of conventional war.

Finally, a word of caution is in order here. The comparison between the two policies will necessarily be somewhat speculative, since the non-nuclear policy I shall consider is only a *type* of policy rather than a specific policy. That is, I have said only what the elements in the policy might be; I have not made a specific recommendation as to how much emphasis each element should receive. Nevertheless, I think that the type of non-nuclear defence policy I sketched earlier is sufficiently concrete to make a useful comparison possible.

Let us then turn to criterion (1). In order to determine which of the two policies would be more likely to reduce the risk of nuclear war, I shall begin by listing the advantages and disadvantages of each policy in this regard and shall then judge where the balance of advantages lies. (The reader must, I am afraid, expect a certain amount of repetition here of points which have been made once or twice before.) First, the main advantage of the nuclear policy is that it might be thought to offer a more effective deterrent against nuclear blackmail than the non-nuclear policy, even if under the non-nuclear policy the US is pledged to retaliate on Britain's behalf. And, as we have seen, the ability to deter nuclear blackmail indirectly serves to deter war. Second, the nuclear policy might provide a more effective deterrent against an invasion of British territory (see p. 106). This would also indirectly strengthen deterrence against nuclear war in Europe. Finally, the nuclear policy might strengthen deterrence by posing the threat, in the event of a European war, of triggering the involvement of the American strategic forces. The major disadvantage of the nuclear policy is that it will involve weakening Britain's conventional defences, and this in turn will weaken defensive deterrence in Europe and also make it more likely that NATO will have to resort to the early use of nuclear weapons in the event of a conventional Warsaw Pact invasion.

There are several reasons for thinking that nuclear war would be less likely under the non-nuclear policy. One is that any war which might occur would be less likely to be nuclear. For one thing, there would be one less power capable of escalating to the nuclear level. And, as I mentioned earlier, the strengthening of Britain's conventional forces would allow more time for diplomatic activity to bring the war to a close before NATO felt pressured to escalate to the nuclear level. Against this, it might be argued that stronger conventional forces might force the Russians to resort to the early use of nuclear weapons. But this problem can be reduced if NATO arranges its forces in such a way as to deprive the Russians of targets against which it would be rational to use nuclear weapons.

A second reason for thinking that nuclear war would be less likely under the non-nuclear policy is that the non-nuclear policy would involve the strengthening of defensive deterrence. Of course, it might be held that this advantage would be outweighed by the loss of retaliatory deterrence. But, as I have suggested, Britain could rely on the US to provide retaliatory deterrence in the cases in which it would be most needed — for example, to deter nuclear blackmail.

A further point which I have not yet mentioned is that, even if Britain were to adopt the non-nuclear policy, a certain measure of retaliatory deterrence would remain. This is so for two reasons. One is that, since British nuclear disarmament would be unilateral, it would presumably be unaccompanied by provisions for extensive open inspection by Britain's potential adversaries. (Extensive open inspection might serve to reveal secret information vital to the effectiveness of Britain's non-nuclear defences.[5]) But this means that there would remain an element of doubt in the minds of these potential adversaries as to whether Britain had in fact dismantled all of its nuclear bombs. The other reason is that these adversaries would be aware of the possibility that Britain could conduct a clandestine rearmament programme in a time of heightened tension, and this would give them a further cause for wondering whether Britain, if attacked, would in fact be unable to retaliate.

Having mentioned the possibility of nuclear rearmament, I should add that, while this possibility would deprive unilateral disarmament of some of its significance, it certainly would not render it an entirely empty or meaningless gesture — as some writers have claimed it would.[6] The difference between having nuclear weapons and being in a position to acquire them on short notice is not trivial. If it were, then the Russians would be just as disturbed by West Germany's *capacity* to acquire nuclear weapons as they would by West Germany's actually acquiring them.

Finally, there are other advantages that the non-nuclear policy would have which are related to the political impact which British nuclear disarmament could be expected to have. British disarmament could, for example, have beneficial effects on East-West relations and could provide the Russians with an opportunity to perform a reciprocal act of good will — for example, cutting back the number of SS20s.

One disadvantage which it might be claimed that the non-nuclear policy would have is that it would be 'decoupling'. Since Western Europe would be better able to shift for itself, the US would be less likely to come to its aid. But this is a very puzzling objection, since presumably the main objection to the non-nuclear policy is precisely that it would *prevent* Britain from being able to take care of itself — for example, in the event of nuclear blackmail.

The conclusion I would draw from this comparison of the advantages and disadvantages of the two policies is that nuclear war in Europe would be less likely under the non-nuclear policy than under the nuclear policy.

Turning now to criterion (2), it seems to me that conventional war in Europe would be less likely to occur under the nuclear policy than under the non-nuclear policy. This may not, however, be because the nuclear policy would make *war itself* less likely, but only because it would make it such that any war which might occur would be more likely to be nuclear — for the reasons we have just discussed in connection with criterion (1). This is a dubious advantage. A more illuminating question to ask is whether the non-nuclear policy would make conventional war more likely than *nuclear war* would be under the nuclear policy. If it would, then this would support the claim that the nuclear policy is in an important sense superior in terms of criterion (2).

There seem to be good grounds for thinking that

conventional war would be likelier under the non-nuclear policy than nuclear war would be under the nuclear policy. The main reason is that, as Lawrence Freedman puts it,

> if the risks of the war turning nuclear have been reduced to a minimum, war might seem in some way 'safer'. This could be described as lowering the 'war threshold'.[7]

Of course, the non-nuclear policy would not reduce the risk of war turning nuclear 'to a minimum', but it would reduce it enough so that this problem might arise. If the problem were to arise, then the nuclear policy would in fact be superior in terms of criterion (2).

There is also a strong case for thinking that the nuclear policy is superior in terms of criterion (3) — that is, that it would make the domination or occupation of Britain less likely than it would be under the non-nuclear policy. For one thing, insofar as the nuclear policy would make conventional war less likely, it would to that extent make domination or occupation as the result of a conventional war less likely. (Again, there is a sense in which this could be a dubious advantage. If conventional war were less likely only because any war would be more likely to be nuclear, then it might be less likely that Britain would be occupied only because the country would be so utterly devastated that no one would want to occupy it.) A second point is that, if the nuclear policy would provide a more effective deterrent against nuclear blackmail, then it would, other things being equal, make it less likely that the West would lose a conventional war in Europe. Finally, as I pointed out earlier, the nuclear policy would provide a somewhat credible deterrent against an invasion of British territory.

On the other hand, there is also a strong case for thinking that the non-nuclear policy would make domination and occupation less likely. This is mainly because, if Britain were to adopt the non-nuclear policy, it would then be better able to *resist* domination and occupation than it would if all of its resources had instead been channelled into the maintenance of a nuclear arsenal. If Britain were to adopt the nuclear policy, then it would lack the ability to mount a sustained campaign of resistance if retaliatory deterrence were to fail.

The advantages of each of the two policies with regard to criterion (3) seem rather finely balanced. Perhaps the balance of advantages favours the nuclear policy; but, if so, it does so only slightly.

Finally, we come to criterion (4). Here it seems clear that the amount of damage likely to result from a European war would be less under the non-nuclear policy. The main reason is of course that any war would be less likely to be nuclear, or, if it were to turn nuclear, it would be less likely to be nuclear to the same extent that it would be under the nuclear policy. Also, there would be no occasion for retaliatory strikes against Britain, as there would be if, under the nuclear policy, Britain were actually to use nuclear weapons against the Soviet Union. Lastly, since civil defence would be both more reasonable and more economically feasible under the non-nuclear policy, it could be expected to shield significant segments of the population from at least some of the harmful effects of war. The only advantage that I think the nuclear policy might claim is that, in providing a more effective deterrent against nuclear blackmail, it would make strikes against British cities less likely. This would be a major advantage if the nuclear policy promised to provide a significantly more effective deterrent against nuclear blackmail, but, given my remarks about the credibility of the American guarantee, it seems to me that this is not the case.

This completes the comparison between the nuclear and the non-nuclear policy. The overall conclusion I would draw is that the balance of advantages lies with the non-nuclear policy. It is only with regard to criterion (2) that there is a strong reason for regarding the non-nuclear policy as inferior; but, as I mentioned earlier, criterion (2) seems clearly less important than criterion (1).

My general conclusion, then, is that Britain ought to abandon all nuclear weapons — unilaterally and at once. On the other hand, I think that Britain ought to welcome the American nuclear umbrella as a deterrent against nuclear blackmail. This, I think, will commit Britain to allowing the Americans the use of certain strategic support facilities in Great Britain — in particular the submarine base at Holy

Loch. It should be stressed, however, that Britain's obligation will be only to aid the US in maintaining a strong 'second-strike' capability. Britain will not be committed to toeing the American line on nuclear strategy generally. To say that Britain should welcome the fact that the US maintains a strategic nuclear deterrent is not to say that Britain should also endorse the way that the American strategic force is developing (that is, towards an ever greater first-strike capability). It is possible to be glad that the US has a retaliatory capability *vis-à-vis* the Soviet Union and at the same time to be critical of virtually every aspect of America's current nuclear policy.

I said just now that my conclusion is that Britain ought to disarm at once. This requires some qualification. The time it would take to implement the decision to disarm at the nuclear level would be measured in years. This is mainly because the dismantling of nuclear weapons is an extremely delicate task. Moreover, as we have seen, the possibility of nuclear rearmament, either before or after the completion of the disarmament process, cannot be excluded. But rearmament can be made more or less difficult, and it should be emphasized that the political significance of disarmament will be increased the more difficult it is made for rearmament to be carried out.

One interesting result of this survey of the arguments for and against British nuclear weapons is that the case for having an independent strategic force is far stronger than the case for either theatre and tactical nuclear weapons or American forward-based weapons. This reverses the conventional wisdom on the subject, which is that, while Britain needs some nuclear weapons, and while it would be a mistake to ask the Americans to leave, Britain does not need an independent strategic force. In a recent Marplan poll, 53 percent of the sample were opposed to the purchase of *Trident*, while only 32 percent were in favour of it. At the same time, only 23 percent thought that Britain should abandon nuclear weapons altogether.[8] If the argument of this book is sound, then a great many people have got their nuclear priorities wrong.

Conclusion

Earlier I quoted a correspondent to *The Times* who claimed that 'hopelessness' is at the centre of the unilateralist movement in Britain. In closing I should like to return briefly to this theme, for I think that there is indeed a widespread feeling of hopelessness in Britain today, though, as I have said, I think it is entirely wrong to suppose that it is the mood which dominates within the disarmament campaign. It seems, on the contrary, to be the mood which dominates *outside* the campaign.

In a Marplan poll conducted in September 1980, 48 percent of the people questioned said that they expected that a nuclear war would occur during their lifetimes.[9] A Gallup poll conducted that same month found

> a deep undercurrent of worry about nuclear weapons, but a worry tempered with fatalism. People fear the bomb and the missile; and increasingly they expect nuclear war. But at the same time, few think there is anything they personally can do about it.[10]

Thirty-seven percent of the people polled said that their view of nuclear weapons was best described by the phrase 'worried but do not think anything can be done about them'. On the whole, the persons in this category were not unilateralists or members of CND: for, if they thought that there was nothing which could be done, they would not be in CND.

What this shows is that there are a great many people outside the disarmament movement who regard nuclear war as more or less inevitable. Implicit in this pessimism is a lack of faith in nuclear deterrence. The problem appears to me to be that, while these people are doubtful about nuclear deterrence, they also believe that there is a serious Soviet threat, and they believe that nuclear deterrence is the only way of attempting to meet the Soviet threat. (In a Gallup poll conducted in January 1980, 85 percent of the people questioned said that they believed that Russia posed a military threat to Britain and Europe.[11]) If this is right, then people desperately need to be made aware that there *are* alternatives to nuclear deterrence. Unilateralism coupled with non-nuclear defences is a course which offers us hope; indeed it is the course in which our best hope lies. When people see that there is this hope, they will perhaps be moved to throw off the paralyzing fatalism which grips them at present.

Recently I heard a television evangelist in the US claim that nuclear war is prophesied in the Book of Revelation, and will herald the Second Coming. By thus encouraging people to believe that nuclear war is unavoidable, and indeed desirable since it is supposed to be sanctioned by the deity and linked with his appearance, this man was able to make his own small contribution to the causation of the final holocaust. It is a terrible and irresponsible mistake to encourage the belief that nuclear war is inevitable. It is not inevitable. But it will be averted only if we refuse to resign ourselves to it. We must take the necessary steps now to ensure that nuclear war does not occur. For Britain, the first step is to renounce nuclear weapons.

NOTES

I Preliminaries

1 The debate took place at Great St Mary's Church in Cambridge on 23 November 1980.
2 Harold Macmillan, quoted in Lawrence Freedman, *Britain and Nuclear Weapons* (London, Macmillan, 1980), pp. 17-18.
3 Ian Smart, *The Future of the British Nuclear Deterrent: Technical, Economic, and Strategic Issues* (London, The Royal Institute for International Affairs, 1977), pp. 33-4. Other information about the dependence of *Polaris* on the US has been derived mainly from this source.
4 Ibid., p. 33.
5 W.R. Van Cleave and S.T. Cohen, *Tactical Nuclear Weapons: An Examination of the Issues* (New York, Crane, Russak, 1978), p. 15.
6 Ibid.
7 Ibid., p. 14.
8 The figure of 48 comes from Paul Rogers, 'Britain's Nuclear Capacity: Minus Trident and Cruise', *Peace News*, 9 January 1981, p. 8. In 1978, the Stockholm International Peace Research Institute (SIPRI) put the number of *Vulcans* at 50. See *Tactical Nuclear Weapons: European Perspectives* (London, Taylor and Francis, 1978), p. 235. The figure of 56 is given in Freedman, *Britain and Nuclear Weapons*, p. 111.
9 SIPRI (*Tactical Nuclear Weapons*, p. 235) gives the figure of 56, while Rogers ('Britain's Nuclear Capacity', p. 8) gives the figure of 60.
10 SIPRI, *Tactical Nuclear Weapons*, p. 235.
11 It may not be strictly true to say that neither can use the weapons without the consent of the other. The double-key system seems to operate in a way which would in certain circumstances allow the Americans to use the weapons without the consent of their allies. Given that the Americans control the warheads, they can in some cases presumably deliver them to their targets without the help of the Europeans.

12 See Dan Smith, *The Defence of the Realm in the 1980s* (London, Croom Helm, 1980), p. 91. Smith claims elsewhere that the *Nimrods'* depth charges, the *Lance* SRBMs, and the howitzers are all under 'single-key' British control rather than under the double-key system. This seems to be a mistake. (See his 'After Polaris' in Ken Coates, ed., *Eleventh Hour for Europe* (Nottingham, Spokesman, 1981), p. 74.

13 Duncan Campbell, 'Target Britain', *New Statesman*, 31 October 1980, p. 6.

14 Lord Hill-Norton, 'Trident Safeguards Our Tomorrow', *The Reader's Digest*, April 1981, p. 37.

15 Hew Strachan, 'Britain's Deterrent', *The Political Quarterly*, vol. 51, no. 4 (October-December 1980), p. 431.

16 It was not low enough in World War II.

II   Arguments for the Retention of Nuclear Weapons

1 In the interest of clarity I shall usually give each argument a name. This may seem a bit strange to people unfamiliar with recent philosophical literature, but it is now a standard device among philosophers. It allows one to refer back to arguments without having to repeat them in their entirety. This can be very helpful when one is dealing, as I shall be in this book, with a large number of arguments.

2 This argument has been enunciated by various Secretaries of State for Defence, including Healey, Mulley, and Pym. See Freedman, *Britain and Nuclear Weapons*, pp. 127-9.

3 Smart, *The Future of the British Deterrent*, p. 6.

4 Quoted in Freedman, *Britain and Nuclear Weapons*, p. 132.

5 They would have an incentive to avoid attacking cities regardless of whether or not Britain had an independent nuclear force.

6 Quoted in Freedman, *Britain and Nuclear Weapons*, p. 133.

7 See Paul H. Nitze, 'Deterring Our Deterrent', *Foreign Policy*, no. 25 (winter 1976-77). For a different perspective on the problem, see Fred M. Kaplan, *Dubious Specter: A Skeptical Look at the Soviet Nuclear Threat* (Washington, Institute for Policy Studies, 1980).

8 Quoted in A.J.R. Groom, 'The British Deterrent', in J. Baylis, ed., *British Defence Policy in a Changing World* (London, Croom Helm, 1977), p. 135.

9 See Joel S. Wit, 'Advances in Antisubmarine Warfare', *Scientific American*, vol. 244, no. 2 (February 1981).

10 Hill-Norton, 'Trident Safeguards Our Tomorrow', p. 38.

11 *The Times*, 6 February 1981.

12 *New Standard*, 29 May 1981.

13 *The Guardian*, 6 March 1981; 18 April 1981; and 30 April 1981.

14 After I wrote this, a splendid letter to *The Times* from Lord

Gladwyn was called to my attention in which he endorses this conclusion:

> Trident, however cost-effective, is simply not 'credible' for use by us alone should we fail to hold up any Soviet offensive in Europe by 'conventional' means. If the North Atlantic Alliance is operative at such a moment, it will be the Americans, not we, who will have to take the fearful decision whether or not to have recourse to nuclear weapons. If the alliance is not operative, Western Europe is indefensible, and the sooner we recognize this the better. For the Russians, who are chess rather than poker players, would certainly, in such circumstances, have discounted the use of Trident before going to war. The idea that we or the French could commit suicide by telling them to retire or face the elimination of Moscow is only tenable on the assumption that we have a prime minister who is mad. (*The Times*, 28 May 1981.)

15 Robert A. Gessert, 'Deterrence and the Defense of Europe', in Ford and Winters, eds., *Ethics and Nuclear Strategy?* (Maryknoll, New York, Orbis, 1977), p. 102.

16 Smith, *The Defence of the Realm*, p. 92.

17 Van Cleave and Cohen, *Tactical Nuclear Weapons*, p. viii. Cf. François de Rose, 'The Future of SALT and Western Security in Europe', *Foreign Affairs*, vol. 57, no. 5 (summer 1979), p. 1070; and Gregory F. Treverton, 'Nuclear Weapons and the "Gray Area"', *Foreign Affairs*, vol. 57, no. 5 (summer 1979), pp. 1076 and 1079.

18 Smith, *The Defence of the Realm*, p. 94.

19 Michael Howard, 'Surviving a Protest: A Reply to E.P. Thompson's Polemic', *Encounter*, vol. LV, no. 5 (November 1980), p. 19.

20 The possibility of deception has even been raised in the House of Lords by Lord Carver. See *Hansard* (House of Lords), vol. 403, col. 1629 (18 December 1979).

21 After having written this I found the free-rider argument being stated by an American spokesman in virtually the same terms that I have used. James R. Schlesinger, former US Defence Secretary, has said that, 'if European governments fail to carry out a European strategy and also let their defence budgets drop, then they will be perceived by US taxpayers as unwilling to bear the minimal costs and share the risks' of the defence of the Alliance. He said that, in the eyes of the US, there is an 'inconsistency between a free-ride and neutralism'. (The *International Herald Tribune*, 26 May 1981.)

22 See Thomas Schelling's discussion of the distinction between deterrence and 'compellence' in his *Arms and Influence* (New Haven, Yale University Press, 1966), pp. 69-91.

23 Robert Neild, *How to Make Up Your Mind About the Bomb* (London, André Deutsch, 1981), pp. 117-23.

24 Emanuel J. de Kadt, *British Defence Policy and Nuclear War* (London, Frank Cass, 1964), p. 55. Although de Kadt's claim was made in 1964, I know of no subsequent evidence which has since controverted it. (It must be admitted, of course, that it is difficult to say what kind of evidence could be brought forward either to prove or to disprove the claim that nuclear weapons provide influence over US decision-making.)

25 I owe this suggestion to Jonathan Glover.

26 See Harry S. Truman, *Years of Trial and Hope, 1946-1953* (London, Hodder and Stoughton, 1956), pp. 419-20 and p. 435. This episode is briefly discussed in Neild, *How to Make Up Your Mind About the Bomb*, p. 118.

27 Sir Alec Douglas-Home, quoted in Freedman, *Britain and Nuclear Weapons*, p. 88.

28 Quoted in Groom, 'The British Deterrent', p. 133. Compare Macmillan's own statement that 'we have been able to make a valuable contribution in many fields of international discussion. I do not believe that the standing of our representatives in these matters — the questions of the bomb tests and the like — could remain the same if we are going now to abandon this weapon.' (Quoted in de Kadt, *British Defence Policy*, p. 54.)

29 See Freedman, *Britain and Nuclear Weapons*, p. 140. On the other hand, Robert Neild (*How to Make Up Your Mind About the Bomb*, p. 126) claims that this account of Britain's exclusion from SALT 'smacks of sour grapes'.

30 David Owen, 'Negotiate and Survive' (London, Campaign for Labour Victory, 1980), p. 20.

31 See Freedman, *Britain and Nuclear Weapons*, pp. 95-6. Now that Britain has decided to buy *Trident*, and is committed to producing warheads for the missiles — warheads which must be tested — there is reason for doubting whether Britain would actually welcome a CTB treaty.

32 *The Guardian*, 27 April 1981. This quotation appears to be a paraphrase of the official's words rather than a direct quotation.

33 Robin Cook, 'Buying a New H-bomb — The Easy Way', *New Statesman*, 12 January 1979, p. 43.

34 Owen, 'Negotiate and Survive', p. 11. Jonathan Alford has made basically the same point: 'The British theatre nuclear forces at present have distinct value in any negotiations with the Soviet Union and they should not be surrendered without Soviet concessions. To indicate an intention to discontinue the deterrent at the present time would also be counter productive in arms control negotiations. If one of the long-term Western aims is to curb Soviet intermediate-range nuclear programmes, it would be foolish to discard the Polaris system or the promise of a successor system before negotiations even get underway.' (Peter Nailor and Jonathan Alford, 'The Future of Britain's Deterrent Force', *Adelphi Paper* 156 (London, The International Institute for Strategic Studies,

1980), p. 36.)

35 Cook, 'Buying a New H-bomb', p. 43. Similar judgements abound. For an excellent if dispiriting survey of the achievements of nuclear arms control efforts, see Bernard Feld, 'The Charade of Piecemeal Arms Limitation', in *A Voice Crying in the Wilderness* (Oxford, Pergamon Press, 1979).

36 *The Observer*, 12 April 1981.

37 *The Guardian*, 21 March 1981, and *New Standard*, 20 March 1981.

38 The *International Herald Tribune*, 28 May 1981.

39 *The Guardian*, 21 March 1981.

40 Michael Mandelbaum, 'International Stability and Nuclear Order', in David C. Gompert *et al.*, *Nuclear Weapons and World Politics* (New York, McGraw-Hill, 1977), p. 54.

41 Quoted in 'What is Pugwash Anyway?', in Feld, *A Voice*, pp. 230-1.

42 For a contrary view, see the letter by Dr Philip Towle in *The Times*, 20 March 1981.

43 This argument has not, to my knowledge, been extensively discussed. It is briefly but forcefully stated by Nigel Calder in his excellent book, *Nuclear Nightmares* (London, BBC, 1979), p. 159. See also pp. 80-1.

44 *Hansard* (House of Lords), vol. 403, col. 1630 (18 December 1979).

45 Quoted in Nailor and Alford, 'The Future of Britain's Deterrent', p. 28.

46 Ibid.

47 Quoted in de Kadt, *British Defence Policy*, p. 52.

48 Strachan, 'Britain's Deterrent', p. 434. Compare Robin Cook's claim that 'the reason why proponents of Polaris are unable to be more candid is that their private beliefs are in flat contradiction to the official rationale. They would justify our deterrent not as making a contribution to the NATO force but as offering us independence of the alliance.' (Cook, 'Buying a New H-bomb', p. 43.)

49 Cook, 'Buying a New H-bomb', p. 43.

50 Cf. Smart, *The Future of the British Deterrent*, p. 5.

51 Perhaps this paragraph will explain why I have had to assign each argument a name.

III   Arguments for the Abandonment of Nuclear Weapons

1 J.J. Martin, 'Nuclear Weapons in NATO's Deterrent Strategy', *Orbis*, vol. 22, no. 4 (winter 1979).

2 Smith, *The Defence of the Realm*, p. 234.

3 For an account of various types of alternative defence which is brief but also more thorough than my own brief discussion, see Michael Randle's 'Defence Without the Bomb' in the *ADIU Report*, vol. 3, no. 1 (January/February 1981). Randle is the Coordinator of the Alternative Defence Commission.

4   *The Times*, 5 March 1981.

5   For information about PGM, see the essays in J.J. Holst and U. Nerlich, eds., *Beyond Nuclear Deterrence: New Aims, New Arms* (London, Macdonald and Jane's, 1977).

6   Smith, *The Defence of the Realm*, p. 169.

7   This point is made by Martin, 'NATO's Deterrent Strategy', p. 890, and by Robin Cook and Dan Smith in their pamphlet 'What Future in NATO?' (London, Fabian Society, 1978), p. 6.

8   H. Afheldt, 'Tactical Nuclear Weapons and European Security', in SIPRI, *Tactical Nuclear Weapons*, pp. 267 and 274. This is a fascinating article (even if it is perhaps excessively technical in presentation), and I would recommend it to persons interested in the problem of European security.

9   Martin, 'NATO's Deterrent Strategy', p. 892. Compare Lord Hill-Norton's claim that 'probably nobody will wish to devastate territory that he hopes to acquire or dominate'. ('After Polaris', *The Economist*, 15 September 1979, p. 22.)

10 Alun Chalfont, 'Arguing about War and Peace: Thompson's "Ban-the-Bomb" Army', *Encounter*, vol. LVI, no. 1 (January 1981), p. 86.

11 Major-General Frank M. Richardson, *The Public and the Bomb* (Edinburgh, William Blackwood, 1981). Page references are given in parentheses after each quotation.

12 Anthony Kenny, 'Counterforce and Countervalue', in Walter Stein, ed., *Nuclear Weapons: A Catholic Response* (London, Merlin Press, 1965), p. 163.

13 I should make it clear that I do not wish to attribute sinister motives to Major-General Richardson. His book gives the impression that his interest is only in ensuring national survival in the event of a war.

14 'Protect and Survive' (HMSO, 1980), p. 24.

15 Adam Roberts, *Nations in Arms: The Theory and Practice of Territorial Defence* (London, Chatto and Windus, 1976), p. 34.

16 *The Times*, 18 April 1981.

17 Of course, Britain would not need to follow the Swiss example of keeping guns in people's homes. Guns could be locked away in local armouries except in times of war.

18 April Carter, 'Alternatives to the Bomb', *Peace News*, 3 April 1981, p. 10.

19 Randle, 'Defence Without the Bomb', p. 7.

20 For a discussion of certain problems inherent in civilian resistance, see Adam Roberts, 'Civilian Defence Twenty Years On', *Bulletin of Peace Proposals*, vol. 9, no. 4 (1978).

21 Quoted in Chalfont, 'Arguing about War and Peace', p. 80.

22 Ibid.

23 Ibid.

24 Ibid.

25 Calder, *Nuclear Nightmares*, pp. 44 and 46. I would recommend

Calder's discussion of these issues very highly. I would also recommend Robert Neild's discussion of the Soviet threat in *How to Make Up Your Mind About the Bomb*, pp. 9-14.

26 Neild, *How to Make Up Your Mind About the Bomb*, p. 11.

27 Cook and Smith, 'What Future in NATO?', pp. 3-4.

28 Chalfont, 'Arguing about War and Peace', p. 82. (Emphasis added. See also p. 87.) Lord Hill-Norton speaks of 'some of Trident's opponents, working knowingly or not in the interest of an expanding Soviet Union . . .' ('Trident Safeguards Our Tomorrow', p. 39.) Mr John Nott has claimed that the Russians look upon the disarmament campaigns 'as a god-given opportunity', and that 'persons in positions of enormous influence at the top of these organizations' are 'neither innocent nor well meaning'. (*The Times*, 20 May 1981.) I could cite a great many more examples of this sort of thing.

29 Hill-Norton, 'Trident Safeguards Our Tomorrow', p. 40.

30 *The Times*, 23 April 1981.

31 *The Guardian*, 20 April 1981.

32 *Statement of Defence Estimates 1981*, Volume I (London, HMSO, 1981), p. 15.

33 Alan Coren on the cost of *Trident*: 'To some, that may seem a small price to pay for incinerating fifty million of us in the space of only a few seconds, no crematorium would touch the job at under two hundred a nob . . .' The fifty million to whom Coren refers are not Russians. *Trident*, he says, 'is the first defence capability to carry a manufacturer's guarantee of its *owner's* immediate annihilation in the event of hostilities breaking out'. (*Punch*, 4 February 1981.)

34 The utilitarian case, and certain objections to it, are considered by Peter Singer in the chapter on 'Rich and Poor' in his book, *Practical Ethics* (Cambridge, Cambridge University Press, 1979).

35 *The Guardian*, 28 September 1980.

36 Cf. Michael Howard's claim that 'the presence of cruise missiles on British soil makes it highly possible that this country would be the target for a series of preemptive strikes by Soviet missiles'. (*The Times*, 30 January 1980.)

37 *Statement of Defence Estimates 1981*, p. 14.

38 *The Times*, 21 May 1981. See also Sir Ian Gilmour's claim, reported in *The Guardian* (27 March 1981), that the prudential argument is a 'myth'.

39 Chalfont, 'Arguing about War and Peace', p. 83.

40 Quoted in Herman Kahn, *On Thermonuclear War* (Princeton, Princeton University Press, 1960), pp. 30-1.

41 *The Guardian*, 11 June 1981.

42 It is sometimes said that the Russians are not interested in trying to fight a limited nuclear war in Europe. There is, however, a certain amount of evidence which may suggest that they are. See Treverton, 'Nuclear Weapons and the "Gray Area" ', pp. 1077-8;

Martin, 'NATO's Deterrent Strategy', p. 884; and Van Cleave and Cohen, *Tactical Nuclear Weapons*, pp. 46 and 73. On the other hand, this evidence seems to me compatible with other interpretations of Soviet doctrine. The claim that the Russians are interested in limited nuclear war may just be wishful thinking on the part of the Americans.

43 Kahn's predictions are reported in *The Daily Telegraph*, 2 April 1981.

44 Michael Pentz, 'Towards the Final Abyss?' (J.D. Bernal Peace Library Pamphlet, 1980), p. 6.

45 See the *International Herald Tribune* and *The Financial Times* for 29 April 1981.

46 As this book was being completed, Iraq suffered a setback in its attempt to acquire the bomb when the Israelis bombed the French-built nuclear power station in Iraq which was nearing completion.

47 'Nuclear Deterrence', in William Epstein and Toshiyuki Toyoda, eds., *A New Design for Nuclear Disarmament* (Nottingham, Spokesman, 1977), p. 85.

48 For information on previous accidents involving nuclear weapons, see Louis René Beres, *Apocalypse: Nuclear Catastrophe in World Politics* (Chicago, University of Chicago Press, 1980), pp. 34-52. Five other major accidents which occurred during the 1950s and 1960s have only very recently been disclosed. See the *International Herald Tribune*, 27 May 1981.

49 See Beres, *Apocalypse*, on the various steps that have been taken in the US to guard against the accidental or unauthorized firing of nuclear weapons.

50 Beres says that the tape was fed into the computer as the result of a mechanical error. (*Apocalypse*, p. 480.) He also provides information on four other major false alarms.

51 Quoted in the *International Herald Tribune*, 30 October 1980.

52 Ibid.

53 *The Daily Telegraph*, 26 May 1981.

54 The best discussion I have found of the strategic implications of cruise missiles is Alexander R. Vershbow, 'The Cruise Missile: The End of Arms Control?', *Foreign Affairs*, vol. 55, no. 1 (October 1976). For technical information on cruise missiles, see Kosta Tsipis, 'Cruise Missiles', *Scientific American*, vol. 236, no. 2 (February 1977).

55 See Nailor and Alford, 'The Future of Britain's Deterrent', pp. 19-22.

56 Ibid., p. 20.

57 Vershbow, 'The Cruise Missile', p. 139. As my earlier remarks suggest, I disagree with Vershbow about the prospect of Soviet defences against cruise missiles. But I see no problem in supposing that the Russians might build defences *and* adopt launch-on-warning. Certainly a launch-on-warning strategy would not obviate the need for defences, for, while launch-on-warning might prevent

the missiles from being destroyed, it would not prevent numerous nuclear explosions on Soviet territory.

58 *The Observer*, 22 June 1980.

59 E.P. Thompson, 'The END of the Line', *The Bulletin of the Atomic Scientists*, vol. 37, no. 1 (January 1981), p. 7.

60 See Duncan Campbell, 'Dangers of the Nuclear Convoys', *New Statesman*, 10 April 1981.

61 Compare Strachan, 'Britain's Deterrent', pp. 433-4.

62 Freedman, *Britain and Nuclear Weapons*, pp. 91 and 140.

63 Nailor and Alford, 'The Future of Britain's Deterrent', p. 1.

64 'Canada's Nuclear Departure', *New Statesman*, 13 June 1980.

65 Lord Chalfont has discussed the just war theory, but he gets the criteria of proportionality and discrimination mixed up. First he cites the claim that 'the nuclear weapon is a uniquely evil means of waging war, since it is a largely indiscriminate agent of mass destruction'. He then goes on to say that this claim 'has a respectable antecedent in the Christian doctrine of the just war, in which the concept of proportionality — the injunction to use in war only that amount of force which is proportionate to the aim which it is sought to achieve — seems to constitute a direct prohibition against the use of nuclear weapons'. (*The Times*, 3 December 1980.)

66 Paul Ramsey, an American theologian, has stated this principle as follows: 'Whatever is wrong to do is wrong to threaten, if the latter means "mean to do" . . . If counter-population warfare is murder, then counter-population deterrent threats are murderous.' (Quoted in Michael Walzer, *Just and Unjust Wars* (Harmondsworth, Penguin Books, 1977), p. 272.) Another writer who argues against deterrence on the basis of this principle is Anthony Kenny. See his 'Counterforce and Countervalue'.

67 It may seem that, as I have stated the theory, consequentialism fails to take into account whether the person against whom it may require one to use violence is innocent or guilty. The theory can, however, be refined so as to take this consideration into account.

68 Jonathan Glover, ' "It Makes No Difference Whether Or Not I Do It" ', *Proceedings of the Aristotelian Society*, Supplementary Volume 49 (1975), p. 185.

69 A great many philosophers have recently argued that this view is false. See, for example, Jonathan Glover, *Causing Death and Saving Lives* (Harmondsworth, Penguin Books, 1977). The criticism of pacifism is on p. 258. Also see James Rachels, 'Killing and Starving to Death', *Philosophy*, vol. 54 (1979); Carolyn R. Morillo, 'Doing, Refraining, and the Strenuousness of Morality', *American Philosophical Quarterly*, vol. 14, no. 1 (January 1977); and Jonathan Bennett, *Consequences* (forthcoming).

70 There is at least one philosopher who argues that, by failing to prevent violence, one can be guilty of a sort of 'non-"violent" violence'. See John Harris, *Violence and Responsibility* (London, Routledge and Kegan Paul, 1980).

71   For further reading on pacifism, see Jan Narveson, 'Pacifism: A Philosophical Analysis', *Ethics*, vol. 75 (1965); Tom Regan, 'A Defense of Pacifism', *Canadian Journal of Philosophy*, vol. 2, no. 1 (1972); and Barrie Paskins and Michael Dockrill, *The Ethics of War* (London, Duckworth, 1979).

72   For one consequentialist argument against nuclear deterrence, see Douglas Lackey, 'Ethics and Nuclear Deterrence' in James Rachels, ed., *Moral Problems: A Collection of Philosophical Essays*, Second Edition (New York, Harper and Row, 1975).

73   The consequentialist claim that it could be morally required to intend conditionally to do what it would be wrong to do is clearly paradoxical. The best discussion I know of this problem is Gregory Kavka's excellent paper, 'Some Paradoxes of Deterrence', *Journal of Philosophy*, vol. LXXV, no. 6 (1978).

74   Richard V. Allen, reported in *The Times*, 23 March 1981.

75   Compare Bertrand Russell's 'Counter-Reply' (to a paper by Sidney Hook) published originally in *The New Leader*, 26 May 1958. The exchanges between Russell and Hook are reprinted in Raziel Abelson, ed., *Ethics and Metaethics: Readings in Ethical Philosophy* (New York, St Martin's Press, 1963). Also see Russell's *Common Sense and Nuclear Warfare* (London, George Allen and Unwin, 1959), p. 74.

76   Russell, in *Ethics and Metaethics*, p. 161.

IV   Summary and Conclusion

1   See Mark Hewish, 'Cruising Towards a Nuclear War', *New Scientist*, 4 December 1980.

2   Neild, *How to Make Up Your Mind About the Bomb*, p. 67.

3   *The Times*, 6 April 1981.

4   See Afheldt, 'Tactical Nuclear Weapons'.

5   On the other hand, if the possibility of revealing vital secrets could be guarded against, permission to inspect might be granted to the Russians in return for concessions on their part in other areas.

6   See, for example, Strachan, 'Britain's Deterrent', p. 439.

7   Lawrence Freedman, 'A Criticism of the European Nuclear Disarmament Movement', *ADIU Report*, vol. 2, no. 4 (October/November 1980), p. 2.

8   Reported in *The Guardian*, 21 April 1981.

9   *The Times*, 22 September 1980.

10   *New Society*, 25 September 1980.

11   Ibid.

INDEX

Accidental nuclear war 101-4, 114-15, 132, 134, 139
Afghanistan 88
Afheldt, H. 141
Alford, Jonathan 109, 118
Alternative Defence Commission 69, 82, 157
Alternative defences 39, 68-85, 89-91, 118, 134-5, 138, 139, 144-50
American 'nuclear umbrella' 39, 47, 131, 142-3, 149 *see also* Trigger argument
Anti-ballistic missile systems (ABM) 26-9, 45, 101, 142
Anti-submarine warfare (ASW) 8, 26-9, 44, 45, 101, 142
Argentina 101
Arms control 52-62, 115 *see also* Strategic Arms Limitation Talks *and* Comprehensive Test Ban
Arms race 49, 59-61
Attlee, Clement 52

B-47 bombers 115
B-52 bombers 9, 102, 115
Bargaining chips 55, 60-1
Bevan, Aneurin 59
Brazil 101
British Army on the Rhine (BAOR) 8, 133
Buccaneer bombers 8, 11

Calder, Nigel 87
Campaign for Nuclear Disarmament (CND) 90-1, 151
Canada 50, 119
Carter, April 82-3
Carter, Jimmy 94, 100
Carver, Lord 15-16, 17, 19, 40, 63-4

Chalfont, Lord 76-7, 86-7, 89, 96, 140
Chemical weapons 87
Chevaline 4
China 115, 117
Civil defence 75-80, 83-4, 108, 141, 149
Civilian resistance 80, 82-5
Clean hands argument 118-19, 132, 135
Cold War 58
Comprehensive Test Ban (CTB) 53-4, 156
Conscription 81
Consequentialism 122-5
Contribution to NATO argument 65-7, 72, 131-2, 134, 137, 138
Cook, Robin 54, 56, 67, 88
Counterforce 17, 18, 100-1, 111, 120, 137, 138
'Countervailing strategy' 100
Cruise missiles 10-11, 55, 60-1, 91, 95, 107-10, 111, 133
Cuban missile crisis 86, 108, 111, 128, 133

Defence Studies Institute (India) 54
Defence White Papers 52, 66
Defensive deterrence ('gain denial') 70-1, 104, 105, 145, 146
De Gaulle, General Charles 97
Détente 58
Deterrence 1, 18-19, 41, 87, 92, 121-5, 151 *see also* Defensive deterrence *and* Retaliatory deterrence
Dimbleby, Jonathan 3
Discrimination, criterion of 120-1, 161
Double-key system 8, 14, 153, 154

Economic argument 91-4, 138, 139

F-111 bombers 9, 95, 111, 131
First strike 20-2, 25, 75, 99-101, 108, 113
Force of example argument 116-18, 132, 135, 139
France 36, 48, 50, 57, 117
Freedman, Lawrence 117, 148
Free-rider argument 39-40, 50, 65-7, 133, 136, 137, 155
Fylingdales Ballistic Missile Early Warning Station 9, 95, 113

Gallup poll 151
General Accounting Office 103
Germany, problem of 62-5, 72, 73, 136, 137, 143
Gladwyn, Lord 154-5
Glover, Jonathan 123
Graham, General Daniel 28
Gretton, Vice-Admiral Sir Peter 71-2

Haig, Alexander 58-9
'Hardening' of military assets 74
Hill-Norton, Lord 10, 26, 90, 111-12, 159
Hitler, Adolf 89
Holy Loch submarine base 9, 131, 133, 139, 149-50
Home Guard 81
Howard, Michael 86
Howitzer 8, 154
Hunter-killer submarines 18

Iceland Gap 92
India 54, 115-16, 118-19
Influence argument 49-52; negative version of 49-52, 130, 133-4, 136, 137; positive version of 49, 116, 136, 137
Intercontinental ballistic missiles (ICBMs) 20, 102
Iraq 101
Irish Republican Army (IRA) 115
Israel 19, 101, 114

Jaguar 8
Just war 120-2, 161

Kahn, Herman 99
Kent, Monsignor Bruce 91
Korean war 52

Labour party 54
Lance short-range ballistic missiles 8, 71
Lasers 27
Last resort deterrent argument 14-29, 62, 116, 136
Launch-on-warning 110
Laurie, Peter 79
Lehrer, Tom 79
Limited nuclear war 31-2, 96-9, 132-3, 135

Macmillan, Harold 52
McNamara, Robert 24-5
Marplan poll 150, 151
Ministry of Defence 6, 55, 81
Minutemen vulnerability problem 20-2
Moral arguments 119-25
Multilateralist paradox 54
Multilateralist's argument 55-62, 130, 136, 137
Multiple independently-targetable re-entry vehicles (MIRVs) 10, 20, 100
Mutual and Balanced Force Reductions talks (MBFR) 56
Mutual assured destruction 76

Nazism 63
Neild, Robert 41, 88, 135
Neutron bomb 30, 121
Nimrod maritime patrol aircraft 8, 154
Non-Proliferation Treaty 116-17
North American Air Defence Command (NORAD) 103
North Atlantic Treaty Organization (NATO) 5, 6, 7, 10, 31, 34, 44, 52, 58, 59, 64, 65-7, 70, 72, 86, 87, 89, 94, 110, 119, 131, 146
Nott, John 159
Nuclear blackmail 40-7, 57, 83-5, 104, 105, 116, 136, 137-8, 139, 140-3, 145, 146, 149
Nuclear Nightmares (Calder) 87
Nuclear terrorism 115, 132, 134, 139

Overkill 57
Owen, David 53-4, 55

Pacifism 3, 122-3
Pakistan 116
Particle-beam weapons 27-8

Pattie, Geoffrey 95
Pentagon 6, 97
Pentz, Michael 100
Pershing II 59, 91, 111
Polaris 4-7, 9, 10, 16, 27, 32-4, 55, 67, 71, 111, 112
Poseidon 9
Precision-guided munitions (PGM) 72, 135
Presidential Directive 59, 100
Prestige, nuclear weapons as a source of 47-9, 54-5
Proliferation 101, 112-16, 116-18, 132, 135, 139
Proportionality, criterion of 120-1, 161
'Protect and Survive' 77, 79-80
Prudential argument 94-104, 132, 134-5, 138, 139
Public and the Bomb, The (Richardson) 78-9
Pugwash 60
Pym, Francis 3

Ramsey, Paul 161
Randle, Michael 83
Rapid deployment force 98
Reagan, Ronald 28, 51, 56, 58
Rearmament 146-7, 150
Retaliatory deterrence ('resource destruction') 70-1, 104-7, 138, 141, 146
Revalation, Book of, 152
Richardson, Major-General Frank M. 78-9
Roberts, Adam 80-1
Royal Navy 92
Russell, Bertrand 125, 129

SS20 Intermediate-range ballistic missiles 55, 147
Schlesinger, James R. 155
Second centre argument 14-29, 136, 137
'Smart' bombs *see* Precision-guided munitions
Smith, Dan 70, 72, 88
South Africa 101
Soviet threat 13, 68, 85-91, 140-1, 151
Statement of Defence Estimates (1980) 88; (1981) 88, 95
Strategic Arms Limitation Talks (SALT) 52-3, 56, 60; SALT I 26, 28; SALT II 56
Strategic nuclear weapons 7 *see also* Intercontinental ballistic missiles, submarine-launched ballistic missiles, *Polaris*, *Poseidon*, and *Trident*
Submarine-launched ballistic missiles (SLBMs) 4, 5, 25-6, 37, 38, 67, 107 see also *Polaris*, *Poseidon* and *Trident*
Sweden 76-7, 93
Switzerland 76-7, 84, 93

Tactic of deception 36-9
Tactic of mere escalation 32-6
Territorial defence 80-2, 84-5, 123, 141
Theatre and tactical nuclear weapons 7, 30-2, 32-4, 37-9, 92, 97, 133-5
Third World 93
Thompson, E.P 111
Top table argument 52-5, 115, 116, 118-19, 136, 137
Tornado 10-11
Trident 10, 11, 26-8, 33-4, 55, 60-1, 73, 91-2, 107, 111, 112, 150, 155, 156
Trigger argument 29-39, 40, 67, 137; first version of 30-2, 130, 133; second version of 32-9, 133, 136
Truman, Harry S. 52
Tucker, Anthony 98

Unilateral disarmament 4, 11-12, 61, 64, 89, 95, 146, 151-2
United Nations 111
US Arms Control and Disarmament Agency 94
US defence budget 58
US National Security Council 58
US Office of Management and Budget 93

V-1 bombs 108
Vietnam 86
Vulcan bombers 8, 11, 59, 153

Waldheim, Kurt 111
Warnke, Paul 94
Warsaw Pact 13, 16, 33, 70, 72, 73, 74, 87-8, 135, 145
Weinberger, Caspar 28, 58
West Germany 8, 46, 49, 62-5, 141-2, 143, 147

McMAHAN: British nuclear weapons

e